THE LAND
IS MINE

OVERTURES TO BIBLICAL THEOLOGY

Six Biblical
Land
Ideologies

THE LAND
IS MINE

NORMAN C. HABEL

FOREWORD BY WALTER BRUEGGEMANN

FORTRESS PRESS   Minneapolis

To Jan Orrell,
Eddie Mabo, and
the Aboriginal People of Australia

THE LAND IS MINE
Six Biblical Land Ideologies

Library of Congress Cataloging-in-Publication Data

Habel, Norman C.
    The land is mine : six biblical land ideologies / Norman C. Habel
; foreword by Walter Brueggemann.
        p.   cm. — (Overtures to biblical theology)
    Includes bibliographical references and index.
    ISBN 0-8006-2664-8 (alk. paper)
    1. Bible. O.T.—Theology.   2. Land tenure—Biblical teaching.
3. Land use—Biblical teaching.   4. Palestine in the Bible.
5. Egypt in the Bible.   6. Jews—History—Babylonian captivity,
598–515 B.C.   I. Title.   II. Series.
BS1199.L28H33   1995
221.6—dc20   94-33755
                                                       CIP

The paper used in this publication meets the minimum requirements of American National Standard for Information Sciences—Permanence of Paper for Printed Library Materials, ANSI Z329.48-1984.

Manufactured in the U.S.A.   AF 1-2664

Contents

Editor's Foreword

It is a special delight to welcome Norman Habel to the pages of Overtures to Biblical Theology. Habel was among the earliest "dreamers" about the series and attended the first meeting in which the series was discussed and planned. I am, moreover, pleased about this particular book because it stands in some continuity with my own book *The Land: Place as Gift, Promise, and Challenge in Biblical Faith*, which was the inaugural volume in the series (1977). Of course, much has happened since that publication.

Habel's study of land takes up the accent upon *materiality* in the Hebrew Scriptures that I had earlier discussed. Habel's book considerably advances the study of this theme, reflecting both Habel's own insightful and imaginative scholarship and the ways in which sociocritical scholarship has advanced in the last two decades. Specially his use of the governing term *ideology* reflects an important turn in scholarship. It is a usage scarcely upon the horizon of our common study twenty years ago, and certainly not yet a word in common or legitimated usage. In his usage of the term, Habel (like most of us) moves between a Marxian idea of ideology as "false consciousness" and a Geertzian notion of theology as a sense-making explanatory practice, not necessarily or deliberately deceptive. Thus, Habel understands ideology as "a wider complex of images and ideas, which may employ theological doctrines, traditions, or symbols to justify and promote the social, economic and political interests of a group within society." Yet he proposes to "opt for a neutral definition of ideology rather than a narrow sense of 'false consciousness' typical of Marxist approaches."

ix

Habel's identification of six thematic notions of land reflects the most recent literary criticism, which is able to identify several comprehensive trajectories or propensities in the text. They are not chronological or sequential, and are not easily harmonized, but they reflect ongoing and sustained passions and interests that may exist side by side and often are in conflict or competition with each other.

It is clear that Habel possesses not only a seasoned understanding of the text and has a vast repertoire of texts available to him but also interpretive skills that include but move well beyond conventional historical-critical horizons. For that reason, he is able to incorporate large questions and rich learning into the turn he gives to specific texts.

The "models" he traces in the book are not for certain seasons and circumstances in the life of ancient Israel, but represent abiding interests and perceptions that persist through the several seasons of Israel's life. Thus the earlier modes he treats—monarchical, theocratic, and familial—embody enduring propensities. The "royal ideology" practices a vision of centralized power, and the "theocratic" notion of power that resists every political force that may be regarded as absolute.

In the latter part of the book, the suggested models are of another sort. In his discussion of the "agrarian" and "immigrant" dimensions of Israel's literature, Habel is, in my judgment, breaking genuinely new ground beyond all our usual labels for such matters. Among other things, Habel suggests that such social vision as the jubilee year pertained in important ways to the actual lived life of Israel.

In all of these models, conventional and new, there are evident and immediate spin-offs to contemporary issues, although Habel disciplines himself against moving into them. The upshot of this book is to show in powerful ways both (a) that the Bible should not be read innocently, and that the God practiced in the several ideologies is a player in Israel's propertied life, and (b) that those old "ideological-theological" positions continue to be poignantly pertinent in the world of contemporary interpretation.

Habel's is a strong addition to Overtures. In celebrating it, I join him in expressing gratitude to John Hollar and to Alfred von Rohr Sauer, both so Lutheran, both so gift-giving to us all.

Walter Brueggemann

Preface

"The land is mine!" This claim, once voiced by YHWH in the Hebrew Scriptures (Lev. 25:23), has been made by individuals, social groups, and nations across the centuries. More recently, this claim has been voiced strongly by indigenous peoples of our contemporary world who have been dispossessed by colonial and corporate powers. Land claims and communal identity are often inextricably interrelated.

Recent claims of indigenous peoples to their ancestral lands have forced existing landowners and governments to reflect on their own claims to ownership and the ideologies that justify their claims. Religious bodies, too, have been exploring theologies appropriate to the competing claims of indigenous peoples, mining companies, farmers, governments, and householders.

In the face of competing claims of peoples to the same land, especially the claims of indigenous peoples to the ancestral lands taken by colonial invaders, religious bodies have returned to biblical sources for guidance. They have latched onto passages from the Hebrew Scriptures that seem to support one position or another. They have repeatedly used the fine works of my friend Walter Brueggemann as a major resource in their efforts to find a solution.

Walter Brueggemann's *The Land* (1977) was the first volume to appear in the series Overtures to Biblical Theology. Walter generously acknowledges my prodding to initiate this series prior to my leaving the United States to assume a post in Australia. Now, almost twenty years later, the time has come for a sequel that takes into account recent approaches and findings in biblical research.

My volume identifies and analyzes six discrete land ideologies found in the Hebrew Scriptures. These ideologies are not reconstructions of historical movements in Israel, but positions that are promoted in the texts chosen for analysis. As such, they are the ideologies that have influenced readers of these texts over the centuries.

Although my analysis of these ideologies has intrinsic value as an academic exercise, the findings of this study should prove a useful resource for those who wish to explore the implications of biblical land ideologies for contemporary land issues and land claims. It is no longer possible to cite the position of the Bible on land as if that position were singular and obvious. There are many competing positions from which to choose. Six of these positions are outlined in this study.

I want to thank a number of colleagues who served as friendly critics for particular chapters of this book. These colleagues include Ed Conrad, Peter Lockwood, Eric Renner, Carl Loeliger, John Kleinig, Jerome Crowe, John Roffey, and others who have tolerated my presentation of early drafts of particular chapters at various gatherings.

I have been supported in this project by my Religion Studies colleagues at the University of South Australia and especially my close friend Basil Moore, who have worked closely with me in exploring issues of social justice and religion. The University of South Australia has also supported me in this project through a research grant.

I especially want to thank my research assistants, Shirley Wurst and Margaret Bolton, whose skills and insights into the formulation of particular sections of the text have been invaluable. My thanks also to Marshall Johnson of Fortress Press for his strong endorsement of this project.

I take this opportunity to recognize the work of the late John Hollar at Fortress Press. John was a student of mine during the heady days of biblical studies at Concordia Seminary in the 1960s, and his contribution to biblical scholarship has been extremely valuable.

This is also an opportunity for me to acknowledge the guidance and affection of my second father, Professor Alfred von Rohr Sauer, who found a lost Aussie student wandering the campus of Concordia Seminary in December 1955, took him under his wing for the next twenty years, and nurtured this rough outback boy into a serious student of the Bible. Von passed away in 1992, and I miss him.

I want to express my deep gratitude to my wife, Jan, for her companionship and honesty is assessing all my endeavors. Her acute consciousness of social justice issues continues to raise my own level of understanding.

I have chosen to dedicate this book to Eddie Mabo and the Aboriginal people of Australia. In June 1992, while I was writing this book, the High Court of Australia passed down a landmark decision declaring the lands of the Murray Island group, north of Australia, to be owned by the Aboriginal people of these Islands under native title. Eddie Mabo was the person who initiated this indigenous claim to ancestral land on the Murray Island group. This claim has come to be known as the Mabo case.

The implications of this High Court decision for other Aboriginal peoples claiming land are far-reaching. The social, political, and religious bodies of this country now have to come to terms with the implications of this decision.

I hope that serious dialogue between the profound Aboriginal understanding of land and the biblical ideologies enunciated in this volume will follow its publication. This dialogue may prove helpful in the process of reconciliation between Aboriginal and immigrant Australians. If leaders of the Aboriginal Christian community so choose, I will release the findings of that dialogue in a sequel to this volume.

Abbreviations

AASR	Australian Association for the Study of Religion
BASOR	*Bulletin of the American Schools of Oriental Research*
JBL	*Journal of Biblical Literature*
JETS	*Journal of the Evangelical Theological Society*
JSOT	*Journal for the Study of Theology*
JSOT Press	Journal for the Study of Theology Press
JTS	*Journal of Theological Studies*
SBL	Society for Biblical Literature
SCM	Student Christian Movement
SPCK	Society for the Propagation of Christian Knowledge
VT	*Vetus Testamentum*
ZAW	*Zeitschrift für die Altestamentliche Wissenschaft*

CHAPTER 1

Orientation
and Approach

In common English usage the word *land* refers to a range of physical realities. Land is dirt, rocks, and sand. Land is the ground producing vegetation, the field for farming, the topsoil of earth. Land is a place for humans to build their shelters and cities. Land is the domain between the boundaries that separate countries. Land is that area of the earth bounded by oceans. Land is *terra firma*.

Even as we name these physical realities, we reflect social constructions of what land means to us. From one culture to another, or within a given culture, land is a social symbol with a range of meanings. We invest the concept of land with a selection of these meanings, some more profound or elusive than others. We create the land we experience; we construct the meanings of land for ourselves.

For the poor Tamil family in India squatting on government property, land is a few square meters of soil. It is space enough to build a mud brick house with one or two rooms. This little plot is the family's hope that it will one day get a *patta,* a piece of paper granting the right to be there. Land is a rightful place to live, to be, to belong. For many such families their hope is destroyed by rich landowners or corrupt officials who appropriate the land. These families remain landless, refugees in their own country.[1]

For the Aranda of central Australia, land is a timeless given.[2] From

---

1. For the plight of the landless in India, see Jesudason Jeyaraj, "Siding with the Landless," in *The Gospel in the Modern World: A Tribute to John Stott,* edited by Martyn Eden and David Wells (Downers Grove, Ill.: Intervarsity Press, 1991).
2. The classic studies on the Aranda are by T. G. H. Strehlow and include *Aranda Traditions* (Melbourne: Melbourne University Press, 1947).

the land the ancestors emerged with latent creative power. They walked across the land leaving trails of their spirit and presence. For Aboriginal Australians the land is sacred, filled with ancestral dreamings that determine kinship, sacred site, and ceremony. All species of life, including humans, are bound to the land. Land does not belong to people; people belong to the land.

For the colonial European explorer, land is terrain to be conquered. Land is arid desert, fierce jungle, or awesome mountain. As such, land is a challenge, a new horizon for human reason to dominate and a fearsome encounter with mortality. Land is territory for managing and mapping. Once land is on the map, the explorer turns entrepreneur and reconquers the land as a vast economic resource. Land becomes lots for development.

Whatever our context or culture, land is a dominant reality. It plays a role in our construction of the world, whether in personal or social terms. Land is also central to the various ideologies confronting us in our respective worlds. Public ideas and images about land, whether traditional or contemporary, influence the way we understand our world and interpret the very land on which we live. Land is the ground of our being.

THE FOCUS OF THIS BOOK

This book is about land in the Hebrew Scriptures. The physical reality we call land may correspond in one text to the territory variously known as Canaan, Israel, or Palestine. In other texts land may refer to a country, a region, a place to live, or a piece of turf anywhere on earth. Land may mean the *ʾadamah,* the arable land on which plants can grow, or land may mean the entire earth, the domain named *ʾereṣ* on the third day of creation.

In addition to being a physical entity, land is also a major symbol with a range of meanings reflected in the biblical texts. These meanings may be linked with economic, social, political, or religious contexts and interests. In some contexts, land is a central symbol interpreted in a particular way and with a particular orientation. These interpretations of land reflect specific ideologies promoted in extended biblical texts.

My aim in this study is to select and examine six ideologies promoted in major biblical texts where the land is a dominant symbol. There is now considerable literature about land in the Bible. This literature deals with land as the political territory of Israel, land settlement and tenure, land as ʾereṣ and ʾadamah, or land as a social entity. A large number of studies have investigated the theology or theologies of land in particular books or traditions of the Hebrew Scriptures. More recently, land has been studied as a topic within contemporary environmental theologies. The extensive literature on these various fields of land study are noted at appropriate points throughout the book.

This study seeks to make a fresh contribution to the literature on land by analyzing how the concepts, images, beliefs, or theologies about land presented in biblical texts reflect a particular ideology. An interpretation of these concepts about land, I would argue, requires that we first investigate the ideological bias of the texts. Any appropriation of these concepts of land in debates about contemporary issues demands that we first take into account the ideological force of the texts being considered.

This book is also about land rights. Although the term *land rights* is a contemporary expression laden with meanings associated with the aspirations of indigenous people today, claims of entitlement to land reach back into distant history. In the ancient world, too, individuals, groups, and nations laid claim to land they considered rightfully theirs. The right to possess or inhabit land, however it may be formulated, constitutes a legitimate subject of investigation in biblical as well as contemporary societies.

As I explore the six land ideologies selected from the biblical texts, I investigate the claims of individuals, groups, or peoples to land represented in these texts. I also examine the various grounds to their entitlement cited within the wider framework of particular ideologies. My investigation of land, therefore, also takes into account the rights of particular groups who may claim, retain, or lose land within a given ideology.

The current literature on land tenure and land theologies in the Bible pays relatively little attention to the specific question of land rights and land entitlement, and even less to the place of the rights or entitlement of groups within a particular ideology. This study seeks to highlight the

importance of this question in the interpretation of land ideologies
found within any biblical text.

SELECTING LITERARY UNITS

This study has been provoked in part by the way isolated biblical passages, usually very brief, are quoted by commissions, institutions, or
individuals promoting a contemporary theological, ecological, or social
justice position. In spite of generations of biblical theology, passages
are still cited in isolation as proof texts with little consciousness or
acknowledgment of the theological or ideological orientation of their
original literary context.

The biblical jubilee outlined in Leviticus 25, for example, is one of
the concepts cited in *A Just and Proper Settlement,* a document intended
to provide a biblical vision for the future of Aboriginal Australians and
their land.[3] The authors of the document are quite aware that the biblical
world is very different from that of contemporary Australia. Yet the
social world of the texts like this jubilee passage does not seem to have
been taken into account in seeking to make the jubilee concept relevant
to Australian society. Is the biblical jubilee truly egalitarian in spirit,
and does it support contemporary models of social justice for land
usage? Is the right of the Israelite family to its land genuinely similar to
that of the indigenous peoples of Australia? Do all people living in a
given land have land rights? This example from Leviticus illustrates the
perennial problem of taking a biblical reference out of its ideological
context and assuming a simple correspondence of meaning between the
ancient world of the biblical texts and contemporary theological or
social situations.

Another problem reflected in documents relating to land studies is the
exegetical practice of studying an individual word, such as *ʾereṣ,*
throughout the Hebrew Scriptures, without paying adequate attention to
the particular ideological or theological thrust of the literary context of
the word, and the resulting changes in the word's meaning. The meaning of land in a given passage is not confined to the immediate sense of

3. Catholic Commission for Justice and Peace, the Uniting Church in Australia Social
Responsibility and Justice Committee, and the Australian Council of Churches
Commission for Church and Society, *A Just and Proper Settlement* (Blackburn: Collins
Dove, 1987).

a particular word, but is determined by the total literary, social, and ideological focus of the context. Land is a dominant symbol related to a complex of ideas and symbols that need to be taken into consideration in any given context.

My study does not focus on isolated biblical passages or pursue a word-study approach to the interpretation of land in the Hebrew Scriptures. Rather, I have selected literary units that represent widely accepted literary complexes. These literary units or texts provide the textual basis for my analysis of distinctive land ideologies within the Hebrew Scriptures.

The analysis of royal land ideology, for example, focuses on 1 Kings 3–10, while also taking into account the wider context of texts like Psalm 2, which reflect the same ideology. My investigation of the theocratic land ideology concentrates on Deuteronomy 4–11 within the wider context of the book of Deuteronomy. And my study of prophetic land ideology is based on key sections of the book of Jeremiah within the total framework of the book of Jeremiah.

Generations of historical-critical researchers have identified numerous possible sources and stages in the composition of such literary units. The relative merit of such findings is now a matter of hot scholarly dispute. Ultimately the present biblical texts represent a completed, even if composite, literary work that depicts a social, aesthetic, and ideological world of its own. It is the canonical texts that address us as readers and with which we are concerned in this study.

As works produced within a particular social context, biblical texts may present particular ideologies that are promoted more or less consciously by the producers of the texts. Our goal here is not to attempt a reconstruction of the historical and social reality behind the texts. Rather, our interest lies in the specific set of beliefs the texts espouse and the corresponding social force of those beliefs as they are reflected within the rhetoric and wording of the texts.

I do not examine the text of the book of Joshua, for example, to ascertain its contribution to the discussion of how the Israelites emerged historically or socially as a people. Rather, my concern is to ascertain the set of beliefs located by a given literary complex that promulgates a social and political ideology of Israel. It is the ideology of that text, rather than the actual social history behind it, that has had, and continues to have, an influence on generations of readers of that text. Two factors influenced the choice of the six land ideologies analyzed in this work. The first is that certain biblical texts, such as Deuteronomy, have become important in the discussion about the concept of land in the Hebrew Scriptures and its relevance for contemporary land issues. The second is that certain biblical images about the land have influenced, often indirectly, Western concepts and ideologies about land. For some immigrants, America was "the promised land"; for many convicts, Australia was "the land of exile."

The selection of literary units chosen for analysis in this study is, nevertheless, reasonably representative of the major ideological approaches to the land within the Hebrew Scriptures. These selections do not include every reference to, or treatment of, land in the Bible. Such a task would require a work of monumental proportions. Land, after all, is such a comprehensive symbol in the Old Testament that it could be ranked next to God in importance.

READING ANCIENT TEXTS TODAY

Recent studies have made us acutely aware of ourselves as readers who construct meaning with the stuff of the text.[4] We are affected by factors within ourselves and our world that influence our meaning-making as we read the text. The questions we pose determine patterns of meaning and understanding. The apparently objective questions that we, as source, form, or tradition critics, asked a generation ago actually created texts with certain kinds of meanings that suited the "enlightened" thinking of our age. We are still unable to completely mask our own ideological interests.

When Walter Brueggemann wrote his now famous work on the land, he stated quite explicitly that his vantage point for viewing the subject was a "sense of being lost, displaced and homeless [that is] pervasive in contemporary society." This sociological and psychological yearning for a stable place colored Brueggemann's analysis of the Bible as itself

4. See, for example, Edgar V. McKnight, *Post-Modern Use of the Bible: The Emergence of Reader-Oriented Criticism* (Nashville: Abingdon, 1988); and "Reader Perspectives on the New Testament," *Semeia* 48 (1989): 1–206.

"primarily concerned with the issue of being displaced and yearning for a place."[5]

Geoffrey Lilburne sought to go beyond Brueggemann and develop a theology of land based on a sense of place. "A recovery of a sense of place," he argues, "may be the means whereby the functions of sacred space can be regained in our secular culture."[6] The context for writing his theology was the rural crisis, land degradation, and conflict over land rights. A goal of his theology is to recover the biblical importance of land. His treatment of the biblical concepts of land, however, is limited, and the divergent land theologies are given scant attention.

One of the factors that has influenced my selection and reading of texts is the social, political, and religious context of the current land rights debate. Today we face conflicting claims of indigenous and invading peoples to the same land. In the Australian context, the invading British laid claim to the land under the legal fiction of *terra nullius,* a land without inhabitants. Britain's right to the land was not based on conquest, treaty, or divine mandate. The land was declared empty, unused, and available for acquisition. The Aboriginal Australians were treated as nonexistent.

Other contemporary questions of social justice and ecojustice may perhaps influence the way I construct meaning in the texts. At this point I wish to distinguish carefully between the meaning I discern in the texts as social documents, influenced as it may be by my social context as a reader, and any application of this textual meaning to social issues of our day. Although I am Australian, I am not reading the biblical texts as pieces of contemporary Australian political writing. I am reading an ancient text from a distant and alien past.[7] I am conscious, however, that I cannot escape my own cultural world, enter the cultural world of the Bible, and be free of contemporary cultural baggage.

Facing this dilemma as an interpreter who cannot be neutral observer, A.D.H. Mayes speaks of a "dialogical" approach in which "understanding is not a matter simply of adopting the life world of the text; it is

5. Walter Brueggemann, *The Land* (Philadelphia: Fortress, 1977), 1–2.
6. Geoffrey Lilburne, *A Sense of Place: A Christian Theology of Land* (Nashville: Abingdon, 1989), 30.
7. An appreciation of the biblical text as alien to the reader is evident in studies of Edgar Conrad, such as "Re-Reading the Bible in a Multicultural World," in *Religion and Multiculturalism in Australia,* edited by Norman Habel (Adelaide: AASR, 1992), 324–35.

rather a matter of bringing that life world into a relationship with the life world of the interpreter. The meaning of the text, then, is the meaning articulated in the context of this dialogue."[8]

THE AUDIENCE IN THE TEXT

It has long been my practice, when interpreting a given literary complex from the ancient world of the Bible, to seek to identify the precise historical audience to which the text is addressed. As an interpreter, I, along with many other interpreters, have generally assumed that it was possible to identify this audience with a high degree of probability and that the message of the text could not really be understood without knowing the circumstances of this particular audience.

Our search for this particular audience, however, has always been a rather circular process. We have scrutinized a given literary unit very closely to discover allusions, messages, terms, or ideas that might yield clues about this historical audience. Evidence of the audience was often almost entirely internal to the text. The meaning of the literary unit was then analyzed in terms of this hypothetical audience found within the text.

But how adequate is this kind of evidence in relation to the literary complexes to be analyzed in this book? What, for example, is the precise historical audience of the Abraham narratives? Or, more precisely, what is the historical audience for that half of the Abraham narratives that many scholars view as the work of the Yahwist? In the past, quite a few scholars—myself included—have argued that the message of the hypothetical Yahwist made sense against the background of the so-called enlightened era of Solomon.

But what do we know of the era of Solomon? The two biblical portraits of Solomon in the books of Chronicles and Kings are reconstructions of the times and figure of Solomon. They are portraits of Solomon the hero and Solomon the villain from periods much later than Solomon. The question then becomes how appropriate is the message of the Yahwist to the historical era of Solomon or, as is more likely, to the later historical period when the era of Solomon was being reconstructed into a literary work?

---

8. A. D. H. Mayes, "On Describing the Purpose of Deuteronomy," *JSOT* 59 (1993): 19.

Recently, John Van Seters has located the Yahwist in the exile.[9] Van Seters has identified clues in the text that he believes point to the Israelite exiles as the audience. But do we know enough about the exile to be reasonably sure of this identification? Besides, which postexilic biblical portrayal of the people in exile is to provide our basis for understanding the situation of the audience?

To argue for a specific historical audience for a given literary complex is, therefore, very precarious and immediately tends to locate the interpreter within a particular scholarly camp. Although a particular and specific historical audience may remain quite speculative for a given biblical text, we do know that the Hebrew Scriptures are literary productions of the Israelite and Jewish peoples over an extended period of time. As such they are productions of a complex social, political, and religious world; a knowledge of this world is helpful for appreciating the broad background to the ideas and customs presented in these literary productions.

All biblical texts, however, remain literary productions, and all literary productions are addressed to an audience implied within the text. We can only guess at the specific historical audience to which a given text may have been addressed at any particular stage of its development. Yet we can discern something of the ideas, doctrines, polemics, symbols, allusions—and, indeed, the ideologies—that are being promoted within the world of the text to the implied audience within the text.

We may not know precisely, for example, when the book of Jeremiah was finalized as a written work or precisely who the audience was for this work, but we can discern in this literary complex the way Jeremiah is portrayed as a champion of a given set of ideas that express the theology of the book of Jeremiah.

We may not know the precise historical audience to whom the Abraham narratives were addressed, but we can discern specific schemas of thought within these narratives that represent Abraham and Sarah in a particular way and that promote a particular ideology.

Biblical works are literary productions that portray figures such as Jeremiah, Joshua, Abraham, and Solomon as representatives of the particular theological or ideological position promoted in the texts. The

9 John Van Seters, *Prologue to History: The Yahwist as Historian in Genesis* (Louisville: Westminster/John Knox, 1992).

ideology is discernible, even though just when, where, or how often that position may have been promoted may remain obscure. The schema of ideas that comprise that position within the world of the text can, I believe, be discerned progressively as we investigate the world presented within an ancient literary work.

DISCERNING A BIBLICAL IDEOLOGY

It is not my intention to enter the debate about the function of ideologies in society—whether they serve primarily as vehicles of social control, as social cement, or as some other purpose.[10] Nor do I believe it is possible to articulate all the social processes at work in the development of an ancient biblical ideology. After all, we are dependent on limited literary documents for discerning any particular ideological stance. These literary documents attempt to persuade their implied audiences of a position reflected in the text. Nor can we return to the historical situation behind the text with any measure of certainty to construct the social milieu of the ideological conflicts in which authors were embroiled.

Yet we can, I believe, discern the ideological stance reflected in the biblical texts. The narratives of the Hebrew Scriptures are more than chronicles of events; the law codes are more than records from legal archives; the oracles and songs are more than aesthetic expressions of poets caught up in personal rapture. Most biblical texts push a point. They seek to win over the minds of the implied audience and persuade those who hear the message that the beliefs announced in the texts are authoritative and true.

A distinction, subtle though it may be, can be made between theology and ideology as schemas of thought in the Bible. By a biblical theology I mean the doctrine and discourse about God expressed within a biblical literary unit that reflect the living faith of a given community. Biblical ideology refers to a wider complex of images and ideas that may employ theological doctrines, traditions, or symbols to justify and promote the social, economic, and political interests of a group within society.

---

10. For a survey of approaches to ideology see Kenneth Thompson, *Beliefs and Ideologies* (London: Tavistock, 1986); John B. Thompson, *Studies in the Theory of Ideology* (Cambridge: Polity Press, 1984); and Paul Ricoeur, *Lectures on Ideology and Utopia* (New York: Columbia University Press, 1986). For recent approaches, see "Ideological Criticism of Biblical Texts," *Semeia* 59 (1992).

The close interrelationship between the dynamics of biblical theology and biblical ideology is immediately evident in the biblical Prophets. The book of Jeremiah, for example, clearly has Jeremiah embroiled in the ugly politics surrounding the fall of Jerusalem. The text records oracles that are not only laden with theological import but also presented as public discourses promoting a forceful ideological position.

Prophetic works, such as the books of Amos or Jeremiah, present prophets as figures in conflict with the ruling powers of the day, be they priests, monarchs, or the wise. The prophetic messages located in these texts are represented as alternative ideologies within the political complexities of their world.

Much biblical theology has been constructed by collecting terms, concepts, and images related to a common theme—like jewels on a string—from a diverse array of sources that reflect divergent ideologies. Admittedly, a given symbol such as Abraham, the promised land, or the Sinai covenant may be common to several texts and traditions, but how these symbols are interpreted in each literary complex partly depends on the ideological edge that is being sharpened within a given text.

A biblical ideology, I would argue, is a complex and contested set of ideas, values, symbols, and aspirations being promoted with social and political force in a given literary complex to persuade the implied audience within that text of the truth of a given ideology. This cluster of beliefs may be intended to uphold the position or rights of a dominant group in society or, as is often the case, seek to counter the dominant position, presenting it as alien to the will of God.[11] In either case the discourse of the text attempts to locate particular social groups within the ideal order of things and relate their position to the locus of power in that order.[12]

An ideology, by this definition, incorporates the factor of contestation, the text being the literary product of the struggle. The purpose of the text is to persuade the thinking of that audience or, alternatively, to

---

11. I do not use ideology here with the connotation of false consciousness as found in the work of Marx or in definitions derived from his work, which speak of an imaginary reality by which people believe they live. An ideology reflects the consciousness of reality that those espousing the ideology believe to be true.

12. J. Thompson, 194. After an extensive critique of Ricoeur, Thompson maintains that "to study ideology is to study the ways in which meaning serves to sustain relations of domination."

condemn the thinking of that audience as alien to the true ideology of the speaker in the text. Although it may not be possible within the limits of each text to identify precisely the "other" whose ideas are being opposed, the dominant images and aspirations of extended literary complexes usually provide sufficient images, beliefs, and aspirations to formulate the basic elements of the ideology being espoused.

In some cases the "other" may be constructed by the text as an evil opponent rather than faithfully reflecting the ambiguities of an actual historical situation. The rhetoric of some texts is blatant and aggressive, whereas others are more subtle and aesthetic in tone. Some ideologies present a frontal attack; others stand without comment like silent parables.

In adopting this understanding of ideology, I am following the lead of biblical scholars like K. Lawson Younger who, taking their cue from Clifford Geertz, opt for a neutral definition of ideology rather than a narrow sense of "false consciousness" typical of Marxist approaches.[13] I do not press for the sharp distinction between utopia and ideology that is typical of the Mannheim school.[14] In biblical texts, visions of an ideal future and dreams of an idealized past are closely related and often inseparable. According to Younger, "Ideology is a 'schematic image of social order,' 'a pattern of beliefs and concepts (both factual and normative) which purport to explain complex social phenomena' in which there may be simplification by means of symbolic figurative language, code shifting and/or overloading."[15]

To this definition I would add that a living ideology, as a pattern of beliefs, functions to promote the social and political cause of a particular group in society, to justify its vision, and to promote its interpretation of reality as truth.

Biblical ideologies, however, are more than single-minded campaign documents for particular social or political struggles. They are complex

---

13. K. Lawson Younger, *Ancient Conquest Accounts: A Study of Ancient Near Eastern and Biblical History Writing* (Sheffield: JSOT Press, 1990), provides a useful critique of the definitions of ideology for biblical studies. His position is based on the work of Clifford Geertz, "Ideology as a Cultural System," in *Ideology and Discontent,* edited by David E. Apter (New York: Free Press, 1964), 47–76. Cf. also Aloysius Preris, *An Asian Theology of Liberation* (Maryknoll, N.Y.: Orbis, 1988), 24–31.
14. Karl Mannheim, *Ideology and Utopia* (New York: Harcourt Brace Jovanovich, 1985).
15. Younger, *Ancient Conquest Accounts,* 51.

patterns of ideas and ideals, many of which may not be systematically integrated but are presented in the text.[16] Moreover, they embrace a cluster of images and symbols that reflect levels of meaning rather than a distortion of reality. It is this complex cluster of images and ideas that is promoted in the biblical text as "the way things should be" in society, whether as nostalgia for the past, a justification of the status quo, a vision for the future, or an intricate combination of these.

Land is the specific material subject that is the focus of our attention in these texts; control of this domain is important to those producing the texts. Rights to the land are therefore fundamental to the ideology being addressed to the implied audience within the text. The rhetoric about land developed in these texts provides the arguments and images deemed valid to maintain the rights to land being advocated.

CATEGORIES OF ANALYSIS

Whatever the rhetorical style of a given biblical text, this study focuses on the central symbol of land to discern how it informs the ideology of each literary unit. To research this land ideology, I have employed several categories of analysis designed to identify the key elements of a given ideology. Although these categories of analysis provide the framework of my research into the chosen texts, the headings in individual chapters do not necessarily follow the wording of these categories in a pedantic way.

Using these categories of analysis involves the strategy of posing key questions that serve to clarify those aspects of the ideology that are apparent in the texts. These questions are not posed in a simplistic way, as if we were asking the texts to answer a questionnaire. Rather, they provide the starting point for exploring particular land-related ideas, images, or social structures being promoted by the text.

The following represents the basic categories of analysis to be employed as the framework[17] for exploring the land ideologies of the texts chosen for analysis:

16. E. Shils, "Ideology: The Concept and Function of Ideology," in *International Encyclopedia of Social Sciences,* edited by David Sills, Vol. 7 (New York: Macmillan Co., 1968), 66–75.
17. Following chapter 8 is a summary of these categories of analysis for each ideology presented in the form of a classification grid.

1. *Dominant images of the land.* What are the dominant images, concepts, metaphors, and expressions that are employed to depict the land? How do these features convey a particular orientation to the land or relationship with it and thereby promote a given ideology? What images of the land does the rhetoric of the text espouse to support its ideology?

2. *Location of God.* What is the location of God in the cosmic and social scheme of things? More particularly, what is God's position relative to the earth, the land, and the peoples of the land? Is God located in heaven, in a temple, in the land, or somewhere else? What metaphors dominate the description of God's relationship with the land? What is the relative kinship of God with the land? Does the ideological focus tend toward a hierarchical, heaven-oriented domination of the land or an intimate, earth-oriented kinship between God and the land?

3. *Locus of power in the land.* Where is the locus of power in the social order projected within the ideology of a particular literary complex? Whose interests are being served by the promulgation of this ideology? How is this locus of power related to the land? Who owns, controls, or has authority over the land?

4. *Charter justifying entitlement to the land.* On what grounds are certain individuals or groups justified in claiming entitlement to the land? What stories, divine edicts, theophanies, or recognized traditions function as charters for the ideology?

5. *Rights to/of the land.* According to the ideology of the text, what rights do a given people, particular groups of people, or individuals have to the land? Whose rights are being promoted? Are any groups excluded from land entitlement? Is the land itself viewed as having any rights or entitlements?

In posing these questions, the emphasis is on identifying the way that land, as a dominant symbol, is interpreted and presented to the implied audience. In some literary units, particular questions may be less pertinent, especially where the social dimensions of the texts are not as obvious.

It is appropriate here to mention the approach of the recent sociohistorical research associated with scholars such as Norman Gottwald, Robert Coote, and Niels Lemche who are seeking to reconstruct the historical origins and development of Israel.[18] Their work provides valu-

18. Norman Gottwald, *The Tribes of Yahweh: A Sociology of the Religion of Liberated Israel, 1250–1050 B.C.* (Maryknoll, N.Y.: Orbis, 1979); Robert Coote, *Early Israel: A*

able information about the various social groups and dynamics of Israelite society. Especially valuable in the context of this study are works that explore models of land tenure in ancient Palestine.[19] These works seek to construct a social and political history of the people known collectively as Israel.

The questions posed in this study, however, do not attempt to reconstruct social history; my goal is to focus on the texts as social and political documents. The texts themselves are a production that is part of a social and political process that reflects the ideology of the proponents. My aim is not to trace the process of this production, but to identify the ideological force of the texts as political products.

I view the symbols, traditions, and ideals of the texts as reflections of the social and political forces who employ theological concepts for ideological ends. The ideals of the biblical texts are not detached spiritual thoughts for the day, but passionate messages relating to the social, political, and religious hopes espoused in the texts. Society and religion are not separate worlds in the Hebrew Scriptures.

SUMMARY AND IMPLICATIONS

This study, then, focuses on land as a central symbol of key literary units in the Hebrew Scriptures. These units are analyzed as literary products addressed to implied audiences from a distant and alien past. The aim is to discern the particular land ideology promoted within the texts. This ideology is researched by using a set of basic categories of analysis; within this framework of analysis, I pose a range of questions to identify the ideological elements reflected in the texts.

In this analysis of six discrete land ideologies, I am investigating the claims, entitlement, and rights to land of particular interest groups identified in the texts chosen for analysis. I acknowledge that my stance as a reader interested in social justice issues may influence my reading of these literary complexes. My prime goal, however, is to discover the distinctive land ideology promoted in these literary complexes, whether or not it is sympathetic with my own position on this subject.

New Horizon (Minneapolis: Fortress, 1990); Niels Peter Lemche, Early Israel: Anthropological and Historical Studies on Israelite Society before the Monarchy (Leiden: Brill, 1985).
19. For example, Jon Dybdahl, "Israelite Village Land Tenure: Settlement to Exile," Ph.D. diss., Fuller Theological Seminary, 1981.

The sequence of biblical texts analyzed in the following chapters diverges quite deliberately from their sequence in the Hebrew Scriptures. This action is designed to emphasize that these literary complexes reflect discrete ideologies that do not reflect a chronological or logical sequence of ideas simply because of their position in the biblical texts. The ideology of the Abraham narratives, which is the final ideology discussed in this book, is perhaps the most radical of all, even though it appears first in the biblical text.

The texts chosen for analysis in this study have recently become significant sources for developing land theologies or position statements on the land rights of indigenous peoples. My plan is to edit a sequel to this volume in which the relative significance of these ideologies for the current debate about the land rights of indigenous peoples will be explored. A consideration of the explicit implications of this research, however, requires criteria for bridging the vast gap between the complex ideological worlds of distant alien texts and our own complex multicultural societies with their range of diverse and often conflicting ideologies.[20]

20. One such methodology is proposed by James Barr, "Ancient Biblical Laws and Modern Human Rights," in *Justice and the Holy,* edited by D. Knight and P. Peters (Atlanta: Scholars Press, 1989), 21–33. Barr seeks to bridge the gap between personal biblical commands of God and universal human rights by arguing that many divine commands in the Old Testament are, in fact, based on widely accepted common practice.

CHAPTER 2

Land as the Source
of Wealth: A Royal Ideology

Royal ideology provided a justification for the control of power and strategic resources; it proclaimed that the king's right to rule was guaranteed
by the deities of the state. A heavy emphasis was placed on the benefits of
peace, security and wealth for the population of the state which flowed
from the king's position in the cosmic scheme of things.[1]

This summary statement offers a broad description of a royal ideology promoted at certain periods in Israel's history. One major facet of
this ideology that has received relatively little scrutiny is the central
function of the land found in key texts promoting royal ideologies. In
this chapter I argue that basic to this royal land ideology are the concepts of the land as the source of wealth, the divine right of the monarch
to appropriate that wealth, and the entitlement of the monarch as God's
representative to have dominion over the whole earth as an empire.

The basic text for my analysis of this ideology is the portrait of
Solomon's reign outlined in 1 Kings 3–10. This text is complemented
by the royal psalms (especially 2 and 72) and selected passages from
relevant narratives promoting or opposing this royal ideology.

My discussion in this chapter involves an analysis of the golden age
portrayed in 1 Kings 3–10,[2] the wealth orientation of that portrait, the
image of the land as empire, the locus of power in the social order, the

---

1. Keith Whitelam, "Israelite Kingship: The Royal Ideology and Its Opponents," in *The
World of Ancient Israel,* edited by Ronald Clements (Cambridge: Cambridge University
Press, 1989), 121.
2. David Jobling, "Forced Labor: Solomon's Golden Age and the Question of Literary
Representation," *Semeia* 54 (1991): 57–76.

location of God, and the rights of diverse groups to land in the perceived implementation of this ideology. This literary unit promoting Solomon's golden age is framed by typical Deuteronomistic passages (1 Kings 1–2, 11), which are critical of Solomon and probably reflect something closer to the perceived political reality.[3] My interest is not in reconstructing the historical situation of Solomon's kingdom, but in exploring the ideological force of the text in its present form. Nor is it relevant here to examine whether the hyperbole of the text is in some sense historically verifiable.[4] Rather, our concern is to discover the ideological thrust of the various images, concepts, and accounts preserved in the present narrative. It is this narrative that has had a significant impact on subsequent understandings of land, monarch, and messiah in Judaism and Christianity.

WISDOM AND WEALTH

The account of the dream vision of Solomon at Gibeon is viewed by many scholars as a political propaganda story (*Königsnovelle*) that legitimates Solomon's accession to the throne (1 Kings 3:4-15).[5] Solomon's request for the understanding required to rule the land is recognized as an idealistic expression of the inner wisdom and integrity appropriate to a genuine son of David ascending the throne (cf. Isa. 11:1-3). What is not so frequently seen, however, is that the text also provides an ideological charter for the accumulation of wealth, status, and honor in the hands of the monarchy.[6] Wisdom is the means, not the end, of Solomon's golden age. Or, as David Jobling puts it, wisdom is "what motors the ideal economics" or the means to "gain other goods as a natural surplus."[7]

After a lavish holocaust of a thousand animals, YHWH is portrayed as appearing to Solomon, who offers his prayer of legitimation. In the

3. Kim Parker, "Wisdom and Law in the Reign of Solomon," Ph.D. diss., McMaster University, 1989.
4. K. Lawson Younger, "The Figurative Aspect and the Contextual Method in the Evaluation of the Solomonic Empire (1 Kings 1–11)," in *The Bible in Three Dimensions*, edited by David Clines et al. (Sheffield: JSOT Press, 1990), 157–75.
5. Siegfried Herrmann, "Die Königsnovelle in Ägypten und Israel," *Wissenschaftliche Zeitschrift der Karl Marx Universität Leipzig* 3 (1953): 51–62.
6. Manfred Görg, *Gott-König-Reden in Israel und Ägypten* (Stuttgart: Kohlhammer, 1975).
7. Jobling, "Forced Labor," 64, 65.

diplomatic rhetoric of a would-be monarch, he employs all the appropriate language of humility and reverence to express his dependency on YHWH. His place on the throne is due to YHWH's kindness (*hesed*) to David (1 Kings 3:6), his capacity to rule is only that of an inexperienced child (3:7), and his people constitute an innumerable host (3:8). In the end, he exclaims, almost disarmingly, "Who can govern this great people?" (3:9).

Solomon's speech uses the court language of deference appropriate to his new position as a king asking for wisdom. This speech is but the prelude, however, to the divine pronouncement that constitutes a charter for the royal ideology represented by the portrait of Solomon in this text. In this pronouncement the emphasis moves from Solomon's apparently humble request for wisdom to the grand array of blessings that accompanies this wisdom (1 Kings 3:10-14).

The glories promised to this wise monarch include wealth and honor, high status among other monarchs, and long life (1 Kings 3:12-14). Of these gifts, long life is linked specifically with continued obedience to the ways of YHWH. These glories are not an incidental outcome of the royal request for wisdom. Rather, they are fundamental to the royal ideal and publicly sanctioned by a divine promise, which is revealed as part of a sacred rite connected with Solomon's accession to the throne.

The combined blessing of wealth and honor is promised elsewhere by wisdom to those who follow the paths of wisdom (Prov. 3:16; 8:18). In Proverbs 1–9, which seeks to represent the orientation of an elite world such as the court, wisdom is the way to material success and prosperity. In 1 Kings 3, that success and prosperity are part of the very charter for monarchs who aspire to the Solomonic ideal. Solomon is the perfect wise one and therefore wealthy.

In line with this elite tradition of Proverbs, Solomon does not request wealth but wisdom, which is considered the divinely approved means of acquiring wealth.[8] Solomon, accordingly, excels all monarchs of the earth in both wisdom and wealth (1 Kings 10:23). When monarchs come to hear Solomon's great wisdom, their visits only serve to increase his wealth annually (10:24). These passages further promote the belief that royal wisdom, like intellectual capital, generates wealth.

---

8. Carole Fontaine, "The Bearing of Wisdom on the Shape of 2 Samuel 11–12 and 1 Kings 3," *JSOT* 34 (1986): 61–77.

At a number of points in 1 Kings 3–10, the great wealth of Solomon is described or implied. Massive amounts of gold enable Solomon to make such things as shields covered with beaten gold, drinking vessels of gold, and an ivory throne overlaid with gold (1 Kings 10:14-21). Wealth and power enable Solomon to build both a lavish palace and a grand temple. The impression given is that Solomon's great wealth is a natural expression of his wisdom, which redounds to the glory of God. Such wealth, used to glorify God and shower happiness over the land, is presented as a legitimate ideal of Solomonic royal ideology.

As K. Lawson Younger shows, the hyperbole expressed in the portrayal of Solomon's reign (e.g., 1 Kings 10:23-25, 27) is typical of writings about monarchs in the ancient Near East.[9] Whatever the precise imperial situation in Solomon's day, the hyperbole of the text functions at a later date to promote Solomon's wisdom and wealth as a utopian ideal or charter for political and messianic hopes in Israel (e.g., Isa. 9:2-7).

It is precisely this combination of Solomon's wisdom and wealth that the queen of Sheba comes to see with her own eyes. She "observes" Solomon's wisdom in the display of his wealth (1 Kings 10:4-5) and exclaims, "your wisdom and prosperity far surpass the report that I had heard" (10:7). And, as if his wisdom and wealth were some kind of magnet, the queen adds her own heavy cache of rich gifts to his store.

Interestingly, this symbiosis between wisdom and wealth also leads to a quantification of wisdom in language that suggests wealth. Solomon's wisdom is, like the number of his people (1 Kings 4:20), "as vast as the sand on the seashore" (4:29). His wisdom can even be measured in terms of thousands of proverbs and songs like so much intellectual property (4:31-32).

This glorification of the accumulation of wealth by Solomon represents an ideal that is in sharp conflict with the law of the monarch in Deuteronomy, which warns against amassing wealth, wives, and horses (Deut. 17:16-17, cf. Ezek. 45:7-8). The warning of Samuel extends this judgment to the royal appropriation of lands, lives, and harvests (1 Sam. 8:12-17). In 1 Kings 3–10, however, the acquisition of this wealth is a crowning glory of royal success as exhibited in the golden age of Solomon.

9. Younger, "Figurative Aspect."

LAND AND WEALTH

Although some of Solomon's wealth is derived from gifts bestowed by visiting dignitaries and overseas trade, the basic material source of Solomon's wealth is the land over which he rules. The land, in this context, includes at least three discrete domains:

• The royal estate privately owned by the palace
• The territory of Israel and Judah over which Solomon had immediate administrative control
• The wider empire over which the monarch claimed immediate or potential dominion

The extent of the crown land owned by Solomon is not specified.[10] According to the account in 1 Kings, Solomon was given Gezer as a wedding present (1 Kings 9:16) and probably purchased other cities according to the Canaanite pattern of purchase followed by Omri when he bought Samaria (16:24). In the same way, David had purchased the threshing floor of Araunah where the temple was to be built (2 Sam. 24:18-25). The temple land and the associated palace lands were clearly part of the royal estate.

The book of Chronicles describes the Davidic estate that Solomon inherits and manages in terms of treasuries, fields, orchards, stores, and herds (1 Chron. 27:25-31). David's conquest of Jerusalem, by his own troops rather than the national militia, supports the claim that Jerusalem became crown land.[11]

Whatever the historical reality, the text of 1 Kings 3–10 promotes a picture of Solomon rebuilding a range of cities, including Jerusalem, as his personal property in which he stores his wealth and houses his cavalry, and from which he administers the "land of his dominion" (1 Kings 9:15-19). Solomon's royal estate is the centralized locus of royal power in the land.

Just as significant in the royal ideology of this text is the political designation of the land as Israel and Judah, a territory that is said to extend from "Dan even to Beer-sheba" (1 Kings 4:25). As such, this land is not viewed in terms of any tribal or ancestral traditions. Rather, the land is

10. Tryggve Mettinger, *Solomonic State Officials: A Study of the Civil Government Officials of the Israelite Monarchy* (Lund: Gleerup, 1971), 80–85.
11. Mettinger, *Solomonic State Officials,* 83.

available territory to which the monarch claims entitlement to meet the royal needs. To this end, Israel and Judah are divided up according to administrative districts that do not correspond closely to the tribal boundaries specified in the book of Joshua (4:7-19).[12]

Whatever the actual relationship between these districts and any prior boundaries, tribal or otherwise,[13] these districts function in 1 Kings 3–10 as an expression of Solomon's wise administrative skills. As such, they are controlled economic units and a legitimate source of wealth similar to administrative districts found elsewhere in the ancient Near East.[14] The land comprises a set of revenue centers for the accumulation of wealth.

Because of the peace (*šalom*) and stability created in this golden age of Solomonic rule (1 Kings 4:24-25), these districts are depicted as providing massive amounts of produce to enable the court to enjoy the luxury appropriate for such a wise and successful monarch (4:22-28). There is no criticism of Solomon's lavish daily menu of "ten fat oxen, and twenty pasture-fed cattle, one hundred sheep, besides deer, gazelles, roebucks, and fatted fowl." In a golden age, such excesses befit the monarch who brings prosperity to the land and who reflects its presence in the monarch's personal world. The land, in turn, is the resource for all the wealth of the age.

Given the right of the monarch to exploit the land as a source of wealth, it is logical that this ideology offers no hint of rights or concerns for the land itself. The function of the land is apparently to produce riches rather than to reflect an empathy with God's feelings or Israel's attitudes.

LAND AS EMPIRE

Beyond the perception of land as royal estate and administrative territory lies the image of the land as empire. Solomon's rule is described as extending from the Euphrates to the border of Egypt (1 Kings 4:21) and including all the region west of the Euphrates (4:24).

---

12. Dybdahl, chapter 4.
13. Mettinger, *Solomonic State Officials,* chapter 8.
14. Na'aman Naday, "The District System of Israel in the Time of the United Monarchy" (in Hebrew), *Zion* 48 (1983): 1–20.

The territory over which Solomon ruled is explicitly designated "all the land of his dominion" (1 Kings 9:19). This expression embraces the concept of empire: Throughout this territory Solomon builds cities, which are the extension of his power and the expression of his rule. These cities served as both storage centers and military bases.

As an empire, the land over which Solomon rules consists of a range of former monarchies who pay tribute to Solomon as their overlord (1 Kings 4:21, 24). Solomon is portrayed as powerful enough to strike a treaty with other kingdoms like those of Egypt and Tyre (3:1; 5:12).

Fundamental to an empire is the establishment of a capital as the imperial center where the grandeur of the monarch is displayed. As Younger demonstrates, "The foundation of a new capital is the apex among the actions of the king as creator. The construction of a monumental capital at the centre of an empire can be compared, for its symbolic value, only to the works of basic creation, owed to the gods."[15]

In this ideology of 1 Kings it is Solomon, not David, whom God recognizes as the one destined to build the temple that is to become the center of the empire (1 Kings 8:19). It is Solomon who builds a grandiose palace with the most luxurious materials and the most skillful artisans. It is Solomon who makes silver in Jerusalem as common as stone (10:27). It is Solomon who draws into Jerusalem exotic commodities and creatures from distant lands—apes, peacocks, ivory, and spices—thereby establishing at the religious and political center a microcosm of his empire and the lands beyond it.[16] It is Solomon who constructs a capital with buildings that are a testimony to his might and dominion over the empire.[17] Solomon is presented as the model empire builder.

The temple is the center of not only the empire but also the universe. People from distant lands are drawn to this center for the formal dedication (1 Kings 8:65). Solomon's prayer anticipates that more people will come to the temple when they hear about YHWH, the god who claims to rule the empire of the earth (8:41-43).

15. Younger, "Figurative Aspect," 168.
16. Carol Meyers, "The Israelite Empire: In Defense of King Solomon," in *The Bible and Its Traditions,* edited by M. P. O'Connor and D. N. Freedman (Grand Rapids: University of Michigan Press, 1983), 421–28.
17. Keith Whitelam, "The Symbols of Power: Aspects of Royal Propaganda in the United Monarchy," *Biblical Archaeologist* 49 (1986): 169–72.

By claiming control over the temple as the sacred center of the empire, the monarch usurps the power of the priests as God's representatives chosen to rule God's people. The priests are reduced to being listed among the officials in the court administration (1 Kings 4:1-6). It is Solomon, not the priests, who is said to offer up sacrifices at Gibeon (3:3-5). It is Solomon, not the priests, to whom YHWH speaks regarding the construction of the temple (6:11). It is Solomon, not the priests, who blesses the assembly when God's glory appears (8:11), and it is Solomon, not the priests, who stands before the altar to offer up the High Priestly Prayer of dedication of the temple (8:22). As an ideology, the royal vision subsumes and suppresses the cultic ideology of the priesthood.

The ideology of the land as empire is also promoted in several royal psalms. No longer are the Euphrates and the Nile the boundaries; the empire is universal, extending across all habitable lands to the ends of the earth. As the prayer for the king in Psalm 72 declares,

> May he have dominion from sea to sea,
>   and from the River to the ends of the earth.
> May his foes bow down before him,
>   and his enemies lick the dust.
> May the kings of Tarshish and of the isles
>   render him tribute,
> May the kings of Sheba and Seba
>   bring gifts.
> May all kings fall down before him,
>   all nations give him service. (Ps. 72:8-11)

The empire extends to the boundaries of the earth; all of the monarchs of the earth bring their tribute to Zion, the capital, at the center of the earth. The empire is a source of wealth for the monarch in this capital and the monarch, in turn, is a source of blessing for all the nations ruled by the monarch (Ps. 72:15-17).

Whether the Davidic empire had universal aspirations from the beginning may be disputed.[18] The royal psalms elaborate in religious language the political propaganda of the Solomonic ideal for future gen-

---

18. Hans J. Kraus, *The Theology of the Psalms* (Minneapolis: Augsburg, 1986), 121.

erations. This royal ideology persists in worship and prophecy long after Solomon's glory fades. The victorious messianic monarch will also have an empire "from sea to sea, and from the River to the ends of the earth" (Zech. 9:9-10).

One of the most telling reflections of this royal ideology promoting the land as empire is found in Psalm 2, where the claim to universal dominion over the earth is given divine sanction. The key lines, addressed to the monarch by God, read, "Ask of me, and I will make the nations your entitlement (*nahalah*), and the ends of the earth your possession (*ʾahuzzah*)" (Ps. 2:8, author's translation).[19]

In the prayer of Solomon, the king acknowledges that YHWH gave Israel "your land," the land of Canaan, as an entitlement (*nahalah,* 1 Kings 8:36) and chose the people of Israel as YHWH's own portion (8:53). These expressions reflect the ideology of both land and people as YHWH's entitlement found in passages like Deuteronomy 4:20-21.

In the royal ideology, the entitlement (*nahalah*) and possession (*ʾahuzzah*) of the monarch are not primarily an appropriation of the land claims of the people. Rather, the monarch has a different mandate. The monarch claims all nations of the earth, not just Israel, as personal entitlement. The monarch claims the whole habitable land, not just Canaan, as legitimate possession. Potentially the monarch owns the whole earth (*ʾeres*) as a rightful land, an empire.

MONARCH IN HEAVEN AND MONARCH ON EARTH

Psalm 2 makes quite explicit the universal thrust of the royal ideology of Israel. The monarch, as the regent of YHWH, the universal sovereign, claims the right to rule the empire of God.[20] With this claim, the royal ideology distinguishes itself radically from other land ideologies of Israel, which emphasized the land of Canaan as the special entitlement given by YHWH to YHWH's people. In the royal ideology, the monarch separates personal rights from those of the people and claims a discrete mandate to assume ownership of the earth. YHWH is sovereign in heaven, ruling the universe from a throne on high, rather than from a

---

19. On the translation and meaning of the term *nahalah,* see the excursus following this chapter.
20. Kraus, 121.

place among the people. The Davidic monarch is to rule below where the "kings of the earth" rage against YHWH and the anointed one (Ps. 2:2). In this chosen capacity the monarch is designated God's son (2:7).

The precise sense in which the monarch is to be understood as God's son has long been debated.[21] What has not been fully appreciated in this context is that the edict of YHWH, designating the monarch as son of God, provides the entitlement for the monarch to claim a portion from God as the monarch's "father." That entitlement is not the land of Canaan, but all the nations and lands of the earth over which God reigns as monarch above (Ps. 2:8).

As son of God, the monarch is the representative on earth of YHWH, the universal ruler whose throne is in heaven. This focus on the monarch as the true representative of YHWH on earth clarifies the image of YHWH depicted in Solomon's prayer. Solomon acknowledges the tradition that the temple is a chosen place where YHWH chooses to dwell (1 Kings 8:12-13). Solomon, however, emphasizes that YHWH did not choose a city where the name of YHWH might dwell but rather chose David to rule the people (8:16). The election of the monarch has precedence over any choice of city; the royal person has priority over any sacred place.

Solomon then emphasizes that not only is YHWH incomparable in heaven and earth (1 Kings 8:23), and that heaven and earth cannot contain God (8:27), but also that heaven is in fact the true dwelling place of YHWH, the monarch (8:30, 32, 39, 43, 45, 49). "Hear in heaven your dwelling place" is the repeated cry of the monarch as God's representative in the temple of God below. God's location is in heaven, not in the land.

Through his prayer, Solomon plays the role of mediator between God in heaven and the people on the earth. God is expected to heed the word of the royal representative and bring forgiveness from sins, deliverance from foes, respite from plagues, and return from captivity to God's people. The prayer of the monarch calls on God to restore fertility in the land when the people turn from their sin (1 Kings 8:35-36). Through the monarch the blessings of fertility, wealth, and peace are to be mediated to the land and the people (Ps. 72:3, 5-7, 15-17). The land becomes

---

21. John H. Eaton, *Kingship and the Psalms* (London: SCM, 1976); Whitelam, "Israelite Kingship," 135.

the source of wealth through the wise monarch who mediates God's blessings.[22]

The monarch's position in the cosmic scheme of things was fundamental to the ideological propaganda of the court. In the royal and enthronement psalms, this cosmic scheme is grounded in the sovereignty of YHWH over the earth. YHWH is hailed as majestic, awesome, and holy (Pss. 93:1; 99:1-3) but, more important, as monarch. In this capacity, YHWH brings peace, stability, and order to the earth.

> He has established the world (*tebel*); it shall never be moved;
> your throne is established from of old;
> you are from everlasting. (Ps. 93:1b-2)

These passages, which focus on YHWH establishing (*kwn*) the earth below or the throne of God above, are not only concerned with creation or with YHWH as a creator God (Ps. 104:5-9). Rather, they provide the basis for believing that the world is a stable, secure, and ordered universe (Pss. 24:1-2; 89:11-14; 93:1-2; 96:10; 99:1). The earth is ruled by a divine monarch who established the world as a cosmic empire and still holds dominion.

The land (*'ere*ṣ), which constitutes the imperial domain over which YHWH reigns as monarch, is the earth below that YHWH has firmly established as part of the cosmic order. YHWH's land embraces all places, peoples, and territories. In this ideology, YHWH is not first and foremost associated with a specific land, a domain with which he has personal affinity. The focus is on God's relationship with the monarch who is YHWH's potential vice-regent over the whole earth, but located physically in Jerusalem.

Ideally, the earthly monarch is a replica of the cosmic counterpart and derives authority from this celestial model. As Keith Whitelam states, "The king's role and functions are the same as his deity, YHWH, in the cosmic hierarchy. The king fulfils these functions on earth and occupies the same position within the hierarchical ordering of society as part of the complex interrelationships of cosmic order."[23] The location of God in this ideology is not in the land, close to the land, or at a sacred place within the land. Rather, God is the monarch in heaven who has estab-

---

22. Whitelam, "Israelite Kingship," 132; Kraus, 122.
23. Whitelam, "Israelite Kingship," 130.

lished the earth below as part of the cosmic order. The monarch of Israel is to be God's earthly counterpart, ruling the earth below and upholding the cosmic order. The monarch as ruler on earth is to be the image of God in heaven.

THE JUST MONARCH AND LAND RIGHTS

Royal ideology also embraced the image of the ideal monarch as just (Prov. 29:4; Ps. 72:1-4). The story of the astute decision of Solomon relating to the two prostitutes and the dead child is presented as public evidence that his wisdom gave him the capacity to execute justice throughout the realm (1 Kings 3:28). He is promoted as the model of a just monarch whose decisions have popular support.[24]

In Psalm 72 the justice of the monarch is to be exhibited in the deliverance of the poor and oppressed (Ps. 72:1-4, 12-14). The monarch is to mediate divine justice to the people and thereby uphold the cosmic order.[25] This vision continues to be exalted in classic messianic texts, where the ideal monarch is expected to promote justice and peace (e.g., Isa. 9:7; 11:4).

Precisely what this deliverance or justice for the poor means in practice remains unclear. Does it mean that the monarch redeems land for the poor in much the same way that Boaz did for Ruth (Ruth 4:1-12)? Does it mean distributing land to the poor rather than to officials or friends of the monarch as acts of royal largesse (cf. 1 Sam. 22:7)? Or does royal justice mean guaranteeing the poor entitlement to land? There are no obvious cases of land rights for the poor being upheld as indicators of royal justice. Perhaps we should not expect any.

Not all references to the poor imply that they have lost their land or property and become landless. As T. R. Hobbs rightly reminds us, the monarch, too, may use the personal designation "poor and needy," not because of economic condition but by virtue of an assumed status before God. Honor and social status may, in some cases, also be indicators of who belongs to the poor.[26]

Nevertheless, "the poor" usually seems to stand for the landless and

---

24. Cf. Keith Whitelam, *The Just King: Monarchical Judicial Authority in Ancient Israel* (Sheffield: JSOT Press, 1980), chapter 8.
25. Whitelam, *The Just King*.
26. T. R. Hobbs, "Reflections on 'the Poor' and the Old Testament," *The Expository Times* 100 (1989): 291–94.

economically deprived.[27] The poor who are sold into slavery in Amos 8:4-6 are probably peasants who lost their lands because they could not pay their debts.[28] The book of Amos seems to imply that these poor should have their land restored by the exercise of true justice in the village gate. But does the monarch ever play any role in this kind of justice?

The poor are not necessarily former land or property owners. Many seem to have been long-term poor families who lived in the cities or the fringes of society, just as Israel had once lived in Egypt. The question therefore remains as to whether those families have any right to claim land from the monarch who clearly had the right to dispense land (1 Sam. 22:7; 2 Sam. 9:7; 1 Kings 9:11). The portrait of the golden age under Solomon seems to indicate that the monarch has a right to land and people; nowhere does the monarch restore land to the peasant poor or grant it to the long-term poor.

Solomon's land policy, as summarized by Jon Dybdahl,[29] involves dividing and administering tribal lands as he chose, dispensing lands he deemed worthy, taking the land out of the hands of traditional social groups, and assuming ownership of the land on God's behalf. Traditional tribal social groups no longer had direct access to the land but had to enter into a relationship with the monarch to obtain land.

The prayer of Solomon acknowledges that all Israel is to enjoy the fertility that the monarch mediates to the land as Israel's entitlement (*nahalah*) from God (1 Kings 8:36). Solomon's golden age, however, also includes the conscription of Israelites for corvée labor as an indication of royal wisdom in the development of a prosperous imperial economy. Israelites are taken from their lands and occupations to help construct a temple, a palace, and a range of walled cities. Such action is not depicted as a denial of rights but as a normal participation in the advancement of the empire (5:13-18). By their forced service, the Israelites help create the glory of the empire.[30]

27. L. Hoppe, *Being Poor: A Biblical Study* (Wilmington, Del.: Glazier, 1987).

28. Max Polley, *Amos and the Davidic Empire: A Socio-Historical Approach* (Oxford: Oxford University Press, 1989), 132.

29. Dybdahl, 120–21.

30. J. Alberto Soggin, "Compulsory Labor under David and Solomon," in *Studies in the Period of David and Solomon*, edited by Tomoo Ishida (Winona Lake, Ind.: Eisenbrauns, 1982), 259–67; cf. Jobling, "Forced Labor," 62.

A distinction is subsequently made between the lot of the Canaanites and the lot of the Israelites in relation to their status as forced or slave labor (1 Kings 9:20-22). This passage makes it clear that the non-Israelite peoples left in the land had no rights to land whatsoever and could be legitimately drafted as slave labor.

The monarch, as the extension of God's authority on earth, is promoted as the locus of supreme power, with entitlement to rule the land by wisdom. The just monarch, it seems, has the right to control the lives and lands of people as necessary to achieve prosperity and as the royal wisdom dictates. Thus the negative portrait of royal policy presented by Samuel (1 Sam. 8:10-18) is represented as a positive success story in the royal ideology of the Solomonic era.

In the light of this analysis, the account of Naboth's vineyard can be read, not primarily as an example of royal greed, but as a narrative struggling with a conflict between two ideologies (1 Kings 21:1-16). The object of contention is a piece of land owned by Naboth. At stake are the conflicting principles of royal and peasant ideologies.

Naboth is faithful to the principle of his ancestral household ideology when he refuses to sell his vineyard on the grounds that it is "the rightful property (*nahalah*) of my fathers" (1 Kings 21:3; author's translation). This ideology holds that all Israelites should cleave to the rightful property of their ancestors and so preserve the divinely designated tribal allotments (Num. 36:7-9).

Jezebel reflects the royal ideology of Israel, which gives the monarch the right and power to appropriate lands as the wisdom of the monarch dictates. She is not necessarily endorsing a distinct Canaanite concept of the monarchy, as many interpreters would contend. She is reminding Ahab that he "rules" the land and, according to the principles of royal Israelite ideology, can appropriate land.[31]

Ahab is apparently caught between the ideal of the strong monarch, who takes whatever lands are needed to promote the wealth of the palace, and the ideal of the just monarch, who upholds the rights of the peasant. When confronted with a strong peasant, he is unable to assume the role of the strong king. Once Naboth is dead, however, he has no

31. Cf. Alexander Rofe, "The Vineyard of Naboth: The Origin and Message of the Story," *VT* 38 (1988): 91. On the ancestral household ideology, see chapter 4.

qualms about taking possession of the land and ignoring the claims of those who might have been next of kin.[32] Elijah enters the scene on behalf of the victim by espousing the ancestral household ideology. Ahab is condemned not only for killing Naboth but also for seizing land that belongs to an ancestral family allotment (1 Kings 21:19). This condemnation stands as an integral part of the narrative account, even if, as Alexander Rofe suggests, the text reflects a late attempt to highlight what happens when Israelites marry foreign women.[33]

In the vision of Ezekiel, the long-standing practice of the monarch appropriating properties rightfully belonging to the people of the land is no longer tolerated. The monarch must confine any largesse to giving his own estates to sons or favored servants (Ezek. 46:16-18). Here, as elsewhere in the books of the prophets, peasant ideology seeks to curb royal ideology.

SUMMARY

The royal ideology reflected in 1 Kings 3–10 and the royal psalms promotes the monarch as the legitimate locus of power in the land and the symbol of social order. The promulgation of this ideology supports the vested interests of the monarch and the royal court. The monarch is promoted as the earthly representative of YHWH, the monarch of heaven who has established the cosmic order. YHWH is located in heaven and from there rules the entire world. As God's representative, the monarch claims all of the established earth below as a personal domain. The land is depicted as earthly empire.

The monarch is also promoted as wise and just. Such wisdom is the basis for material wealth and success in ruling the empire. The land is primarily a source of wealth that is concentrated in the court and expected to flow to the people. The land of Judah and Israel can be used by the monarch as deemed necessary to promote the glory of the

---

32. Dybdahl maintains that because Ahab and Naboth were both natives of Jezreel and probably kin, Ahab had grounds for taking the land after Naboth's death. This ignores, however, the fact that Elijah condemns Ahab's act of land seizure.
33. Rofe, 102.

empire. The land, from Dan to Beer-sheba, belongs to the sovereign to organize, tax, and exploit as the sovereign chooses.

The charters for the monarch's status and entitlement in this ideology are located in the dream vision to Solomon (1 Kings 3:5-14), the divine choice of Solomon to build the temple (8:19), and the divine pronouncement of the monarch as the son of God possessing the right to inherit the empire of the earth (Psalm 2).

The people, as a whole, have a right to the land as their entitlement from God. The monarch has a higher entitlement, which extends to the whole earth. The rights of the ancestral families of the land are subsumed under the rights of the monarch to appropriate land needed to increase the wealth of the court. The poor and the Canaanite have no right to land; they can be made slaves of the empire at the will of the monarch.

Excursus

on *naḥalah*

One of the key terms employed in the land ideologies discussed in this study is *naḥalah*. Most standard translations still render the term "inheritance," which, as scholars such as Jon Dybdahl have shown, is quite misleading in most passages.[1] In the vast majority of cases when the term is used in the texts under analysis, there is no connection with the legal transfer of land or property from parent to child, or ancestor to progeny, as an inheritance. The demise of a parent is not integral to the import of the verb *nḥl* or the noun *naḥalah*.

In his dissertation on the concept of inheritance in the Old Testament, Arthur Brown followed the lead of previous scholars and sought to establish "inheritance" as basic to the meaning of *naḥalah* and the verb *nḥl* in texts referring to the familial social customs of Israel.[2] Typical passages he cites include Genesis 31:14; Job 42:15; Ruth 4:5-6; Judges 11:2; Micah 2:2; and Proverbs 13:22; 19:14; 20:21. More recently, Christopher Wright has reaffirmed that the context of familial inheritance is basic to the meaning of *naḥalah*.[3]

Although Brown's analysis can be challenged in reference to specific texts where the meaning "inheritance" is clearly inappropriate (as in Prov. 20:21), the question at issue is whether "inheritance" is the primary meaning of the term and all other meanings and usages are applied, or whether another meaning is primary and the isolated passages that make a link with familial property are derived and secondary.

The research of R. O. Forshey sought to establish that the term *naḥalah* was linked originally to a feudal rather than a nomadic social context.[4] According to

1. Dybdahl, 54ff.
2. Arthur M. Brown, "The Concept of Inheritance in the Old Testament," Ph.D. diss., Columbia University, 1965, 8ff.
3. Christopher J. H. Wright, *God's People in God's Land: Family, Land and Property in the Old Testament* (Grand Rapids: Wm. B. Eerdmans Publishing Co., 1990), 19.
4. R. O. Forshey, "The Hebrew Root *NHL* and Its Semitic Cognates," Ph.D. diss., Harvard University, 1972, 2ff.

33

this model, the feudal ruler gave devoted servants a *naḥalah* as a grant, especially for years of military service. In his analysis, Forshey is critical of Friedrich Horst[5] for assuming a basic nomadic model associated with communal landholding in determining the meaning of the term.[6]

Gillis Gerleman also poses the question of whether the concept of inheritance is appropriate to describe the land of Canaan as a gift or grant. He views the basic meaning of *naḥalah* as *Wohnsitz* or "dwelling place" and a derived meaning as *Wohnrecht* or "living right/privilege."[7]

As Dybdahl points out, in the vast majority of cases in the books of Joshua and Numbers (where the term appears most frequently), "there is no reference to death or to the passing on from one member of the family to another." Further, he argues, the term *naḥalah* "often seems to have a connotation of referring to a part/share/portion of land."[8] My research in this study supports Dybdahl's basic position, but with the modification that the verb *nḥl* has to do with the division of property, land being the property most frequently divided. The parallelism of Micah 2:2, for example, suggests that the *naḥalah* of a person includes the ancestral household (*bet*) and not the land alone (cf. Gen. 31:14-16; Prov. 19:14).

This basic definition of *naḥalah* is confirmed by its frequent association with the root *ḥlq*, "to divide/allot," and its nominal form, *ḥeleq*, "lot/portion/share" (e.g., Josh. 18:7; 19:1, 9; Num. 18:20). In the book of Joshua the act of dividing (*ḥlq*) the land results in each tribe and ancestral family obtaining its *naḥalah* (Josh. 18:2). Each tribe and ancestral family obtains its allotment, the holding to which it is entitled by virtue of the divinely approved land grant process (cf. Josh. 14:2-5).

The terms *naḥalah* and *ḥeleq* are repeatedly paired in connection with the Levites who have no "portion" or "share" in the land. Instead, their "portion" is variously designated as YHWH (Num. 18:20; Deut. 10:9; 18:1-2), the priesthood of YHWH (Josh. 18:7; cf. Num. 18:24), or towns with pasture lands (Josh. 14:4; cf. 21:3). For YHWH to be designated an "inheritance" makes no obvious sense; there is no handing down of God to the Levites upon the death of a deity.

Dybdahl argues, on the basis of Numbers 16:14, where Dathan and Abiram complain that Moses has not granted them a *naḥalah* of field or vineyard, that in the books of Joshua and Numbers the basic meaning of *naḥalah* is "a right to a

---

5. Friedrich Horst, "Zwei Begriffe fur Eigentum (Besitz): *naḥala* und *'aḥuzza,"* in *Verbannung und Heimkehr,* edited by A. Fuschke (Tübingen: J. C. B. Mohr, 1961), 135–56.
6. Forshey, 30.
7. Gillis Gerleman, "Nutzrecht und Wohnrecht: zur Bedeutung von 'Achuzah und Nachalah.'" *ZAW* 89 (1977): 313–25.
8. Dybdahl, 59.

share of land for living and farming."[9] To restrict the social context to the agricultural domain is unwarranted, although the association with livelihood is reasonable in many passages. In those passages that speak of Israel as YHWH's *naḥalah*, it seems rather forced to speak of Israel as YHWH's livelihood (e.g., Deut. 4:20; 32:9).

The primordial action of Elyon dividing up the peoples of earth according to the number of the "sons of God" in the celestial council results in Jacob being YHWH's *naḥalah* (Deut. 32:8-9). Once again *naḥalah* is parallel to *ḥeleq*. Israel is YHWH's rightful portion or chosen share among the peoples of the earth.

In this instance, as in many others, it is the action of determining the *naḥalah* of a deity, a people, a tribe, an ancestral family, or an individual that makes the resultant portion a rightful one, whether that action is viewed in legal, social, or religious terms. A *naḥalah* is a rightful share or allotment, an approved entitlement to land, property, or people. This allotment may be established by a formal act of the head of the household (Job 42:15), by the divinely approved process of lots (Josh. 14.2), by a decision of God in the heavenly council (Deut. 32:8-9), or through an action of God in history (Deut. 4:20).

A *naḥalah*, in its primary meaning, is not something simply handed down from generation to generation, but the entitlement or rightful property of a party that is legitimated by a recognized social custom, legal process, or divine charter. Only in familial contexts, where the head of the ancestral household gives the *naḥalah* to children, does a derived meaning of "inheritance" fit this term (Ruth 4:5-6, 10; Judg. 11:2; Num. 27:7).

The frequent use of the verb *ntn*, "to give/grant," in connection with the noun *naḥalah* is significant. Dathan and Abiram complain because they have not been assigned a land grant of fields or vineyards (Num. 16:14). The Levites are granted tithes as the *naḥalah* for their livelihood (Num. 18:26) and cities as the *naḥalah* for their residences (Josh. 21:3). Land grants are made to the ancestral families of Israel by lot, but a grant is assigned to the daughters of Zelophehad by special request (Num. 36:2). The entire land of Canaan is a grant, a *naḥalah* given to the Israelites by YHWH as their rightful possession (Deut. 4:21; 12:9; and often). The "giving" of a *naḥalah*, therefore, seems to be equivalent to a legal grant of land or property.[10]

In the analysis of land ideologies in this book, I generally avoid the inappropriate rendering "inheritance" and use, as appropriate, expressions such as portion, share, entitlement, allotment, and rightful property.

---

9. Dybdahl, 62.
10. On the legal connotation of *ntn* in such contexts, see Harry M. Orlinsky, "The Biblical Concept of the Land of Israel: Cornerstone of the Covenant between God and Israel," in *The Land of Israel: Jewish Perspectives,* edited by L. A. Hoffman (Notre Dame, Ind.: University of Notre Dame Press, 1986), 27-64.

CHAPTER 3

Land as Conditional Grant:
A Theocratic Ideology

The book of Deuteronomy is a political document. Following a lead
given in Josephus, S. Dean McBride analyzes the book as "a divinely
authorised and comprehensive polity" (*politeia*). As such, the work is
the "charter for a constitutional theocracy."[1] According to McBride,

> While the Deuteronomic Torah may be deeply indebted to such [ancient
> Near Eastern] traditions, it is identical in form, content, and purpose with
> none of them. With it, something quite distinctive seems to have been cre-
> ated, a comprehensive social charter, perhaps uniquely appropriate to the
> peculiar covenant identity that Israel claimed for itself.[2]

Given the political and social dimension of this work, what ideology
of the land is being promoted as part of this social charter? In exploring
this question, we shall focus especially on the exhortations of
Deuteronomy 4–11, recognizing that these speeches are closely related
to the wider framework of the book, which incorporates the constitutional laws of the land in Deuteronomy 12–26.

An appreciation of the land ideology of Deuteronomy requires that
we take into account the role of YHWH as the deity allocating the land,
the land as a grant or allocation by that deity to Israel, the land treaty
that establishes the place of the land in the polity established by
YHWH, and the social order espoused for the land.

---

1. S. Dean McBride, "Polity of the Covenant People," *Interpretation* 41 (1987): 229, 238.
2. McBride, 237; Mayes, "On describing the purpose of Deuteronomy," surveys some of
the alternative theories about the purpose of Deuteronomy and reflects on the position of
McBride in terms of contemporary hermeneutical theory.

YHWH, THE LANDOWNER

YHWH is identified as the owner and ruler over the land in which Israel is to live under the polity or *torah* outlined in Deuteronomy. This landowner is not, however, a local deity—who might be viewed as the divine ruler over Canaan—with which Israel must deal. The image of YHWH promoted in Deuteronomy is that of a universal monarch who controls vast domains, of which Canaan happens to be one. YHWH is said to control more extensive domains than great rulers such as Nebuchadnezzar, Darius II, and their corresponding patron deities. YHWH, in fact, claims to be ruler over the heavens above and the earth below. YHWH is portrayed as ruler of all lands and God over all nations. YHWH is God of gods, controlling the world from on high (Deut. 4:39; 10:14, 17).

As YHWH is viewed as a relatively unknown deity on the ancient Near Eastern scene, this claim is not widely recognized among the other nations and is only in the process of being revealed fully to Israel. By whatever name this deity may have been known to a handful of Israel's ancestors, YHWH is recognized in Deuteronomy as a newcomer to the world scene who is in the process of establishing credibility and authority. The allocation of a piece of YHWH's universal domain to Israel and the establishment of Israel as a people in that land are crucial steps in the public demonstration of YHWH's sovereignty over all lands. In Deuteronomy, the text presents YHWH as a deity seeking to prove these claims to universal dominion.[3]

The rulers of great empires, like Tiglathpileser of Assyria or Nebuchadnezzar of Babylon, used powerful armies to conquer lands and establish their authority over those lands. In some cases they also took ethnic groups from one conquered area and relocated them in another region of the empire. The goal, it seems, was to disempower and assimilate these ethnic groups. After the fall of Samaria (722 B.C.E.), a group of Northern Israelites suffered such a fate under the Assyrian rulers. Although a regional governor may have been placed in charge of such groups, the ruler of the empire was not personally concerned about these conquered peoples as vehicles of personal fame. A

---

3. Ronald E. Clements, *Deuteronomy* (Sheffield: Academic Press, 1989), chapter 5, provides a clear portrait of YHWH as a distant, transcendent, and universal ruler.

ruler's greatness was evident in the obvious political and military might wielded over the empire.

According to Deuteronomy, YHWH's mode for demonstrating authority as ruler of all lands differs radically from the preceding imperial model. YHWH initiates the unprecedented action of selecting a cluster of people who were living as slaves in Egypt to be the nation through whom YHWH's rulership is to be revealed to the world. These slaves, known in the biblical text as Israelites, are chosen for this role from all the peoples of the earth (Deut. 7:6). This is made explicit in the following text: "Although heaven and the heaven of heavens belong to the LORD your God, the earth with all that is in it, yet the LORD set his heart in love on your ancestors alone and chose you, their descendants after them, out of all the peoples" (Deut. 10:14-15).

The process of liberating Israel from Egypt is commonly acclaimed in Deuteronomy as the mighty act that placed YHWH on the world map as a powerful deity—at least in Israel's eyes. The exodus event happened so that Israel might "acknowledge" (*yadaᶜ*) that YHWH is indeed God (Deut. 4:35; cf. 5:6, 15; 6:12, 21-22; 7:18-19; 8:14; 11:2-4). Elsewhere in the Pentateuch, too, the exodus event is considered public proof of YHWH's capacity to rescue a people from a mighty empire like Egypt; it is considered to demonstrate divine authority. The Song of Miriam (Exodus 15) has long been recognized as a celebration of YHWH's divine kingship.[4]

Just as crucial in the public proving of YHWH as God and ruler over all lands is the process of settling the Israelites in their allocated land (Deut. 4:37-39). The conquest and occupation of Canaan are not merely the extension of a great ruler's empire, but the basis for recognizing that YHWH is the supreme God of the universe (4:39). The land of Canaan is a test case. YHWH's claim to dominion over all lands is to be demonstrated, it seems, by a capacity to deliver the allocated territory of Canaan into the hands of the chosen people. YHWH's identity and authority as ruler are linked to YHWH's capacity to conquer the land allocated to Israel.

The Israelites are to recognize YHWH as their leader by those mighty

---

4. Norman Habel, *Yahweh Versus Baal* (New York: Bookman Associates, 1964), chapter 3; Frank M. Cross, *Canaanite Myth and Hebrew Epic* (Cambridge: Harvard University Press, 1973), chapters 5 and 6.

feats that are the mark of an invincible warrior. YHWH's prowess is revealed by traveling ahead of Israel as a "devouring fire" that defeats all people in its path (Deut. 9:1-3). It is ultimately YHWH, and not Israel, who achieves victory over the nations of Canaan (7:1, 17-21; 9:4-6; 20:4). Israel is given no opportunity to claim any of the glory for conquering the allocated land. YHWH is the invincible monarch, the recognized ruler of the land. YHWH is to be acclaimed as such through mighty conquering deeds in Canaan.

This recognition of YHWH as ruler is not to be confined to Israel. Egypt is depicted as watching to see whether in fact YHWH has the capacity to settle the Israelites in the land allocated to them (Deut. 9:25-28). Ultimately, because of YHWH's military prowess, the Israelites will be a feared people wherever they go (2:25; 7:23-24; 11:25). And their land will extend far beyond the borders of the territory of Canaan as assigned to the twelve tribes, according to the allotments outlined in the book of Joshua (Deut. 11:24). Then YHWH's sovereignty will be proven to all; the granting of land will have vindicated YHWH's claim. When Israel experiences the blessings of YHWH in Canaan, as territory under treaty, "all peoples of the earth" will know that YHWH is Israel's ruler and respond in fear (28:10).

LAND AS GIFT

Within the ideological framework of YHWH's claim to absolute dominion, the land of Canaan is relentlessly promoted as a gift or grant. In theological terms, this concept is usually interpreted as an expression of unequivocal divine grace. In social and political terms, however, the continuous reminder that the Israelites who invaded the land have not earned the land is designed to create a sense of total indebtedness and dependency on YHWH as the universal ruler and land-giver. Canaan is YHWH's land grant to Israel.

The rhetoric of God "giving" or "granting" (*natan*) the land (*'ereṣ*, *'adamah*) is found throughout Deuteronomy.[5] YHWH gives rest and

5. E. W. Davies, "Land: Its Rights and Privileges," in *The World of Ancient Israel: Sociological, Anthropological, and Political Perspectives,* edited by Robert Clements (Cambridge: Cambridge University Press, 1989), 350–51; Patrick D. Miller, "The Gift of God: The Deuteronomic Theology of the Land," *Interpretation* 23 (1969): 451–65; Van Seters, *Prologue to History,* 229–30, contrary to Lothar Perlitt, "Motive und Schichten der Landtheologie im Deuteronomium," in *Das Land Israels in biblischer Zeit,* edited by

entitlement (Deut. 12:9-10), blessings (12:15), flocks and herds (12:21), crops and rain (11:14-15), towns (13:12), gates (16:5), and sons and daughters (28:53). The land, however, is the primary and crucial gift in the ideology of Deuteronomy.

To appreciate the full force of this gift, it is helpful to trace the progression of divine acts that constitute the granting of land as a new territory for Israel to possess. These can be discerned from the progression of verbs employed in connection with the process of Israel's settlement.

The first stage in Israel's acceptance of this land grant is to "go in and possess" (bw' and yaraš) the land (Deut. 1:8; 4:1; 6:18; 7:1; 8:1; 10:11; 11:8, 29). A more accurate rendering would perhaps be "invade and occupy." The land Israel is to invade and occupy is the land that YHWH, owner of all lands, "gives" to Abraham, Isaac, and Jacob and to their descendants (6:10, 18; 7:13; 8:1; 10:11; 11:9). The granting of land has occupation of the land as its goal. This is the land "I am giving them to occupy" (3:18; 5:31; 12:1; 17:14; 19:1, 14). To occupy or possess the land seems to mean laying claim to the territory that has been allocated by the ruler of all the earth.

Whether the ancestors cited in these texts of Deuteronomy refer to Abraham, Isaac, and Jacob; the Exodus generation of Israelites, as John Van Seters argues;[6] or to a more general concept of ancestors, the "promise to the ancestors" functions as an ideological doctrine justifying the occupation of Canaan.

The second stage involves clearing out (našal) and dispossessing (yaraš) the existing inhabitants of the land (Deut. 7:1, 2, 20, 22, 24; 4:38; 9:1, 3, 4; 11:23). This stage is also the work of YHWH as the universal land-giver (9:3). The Israelites cannot claim that they have any right to the land by virtue of their mighty exploits or their righteous ways. On the contrary, they receive the land by default; the wickedness of the original inhabitants demanded their expulsion (9:4-7). Here again the gift ideology fosters an attitude of total indebtedness and dependency on the land-giver (8:17, 18) and a corresponding negation of anything Canaanite. YHWH is to get all the glory and all Israel's gratitude; the indigenous Canaanites are to get nothing.

G. Strecker (Göttingen: Vandenhoeck & Ruprecht, 1983), 46–58. Perlitt argues that the theology of the land as a conditional gift belongs to the oldest level of tradition in the laws of Deuteronomy but was not linked to the promise to the ancestors.
6. Van Seters, *Prologue to History,* 233.

The third stage involves settling (*yašab*) in the land (Deut. 11:31; 12:10; 17:14; 26:1; 30:20) and finding rest (*nwh*) from enemies (3:20; 12:9, 10; 25:19). It is God who gives rest after the process of occupation and conquest is complete. Rest marks the completion of the land grants; it is the time to settle down and celebrate the gift of land and the gifts from the harvest (26:1-11).

> From beginning to end, Israel's entry, occupation and settlement of the allocated land is viewed as God's gift. Israel owes everything to her YHWH, her land-giver. The full force of this gift becomes apparent when we recognise that the verb *ntn* may carry the legal force not simply of "give" but "assign, deed, transfer, convey," and that it was used as a legal, real estate term to indicate transfer of ownership of or title to a piece of property.[7]

The owner of all lands, who assigns peoples to their lands, has assigned or deeded Canaan over as Israel's national territory. Canaan is Israel's legally allocated territory; Canaan is a land grant. In the tradition preserved in another text of Deuteronomy, this allocation is not a decision of YHWH at a particular point in history but part of a primordial ordering of all lands. In the beginning, YHWH, who is apparently identified with the ancient high god, El Elyon, assigns Israel to be a personal portion (Deut. 32:7-9).

THE LAND AS GOOD

The theme of indebtedness, which is integral to the ideology of Deuteronomy, is also promoted in the way the land itself is described. The land is good (*tob,* Deut. 4:21-22; 8:7-10), a land flowing with milk and honey (6:3; 11:9). An undeserved gift from a great and generous landowner is of necessity something glorious and good. An appreciative and privileged people is expected to view it thus, whatever may have been the historical realities of life in the hill country that the Israelites first occupied.

A lyrical portrait of the land's goodness is given in Deuteronomy 8:7-10:

> For the LORD your God is bringing you into a good land, a land with flowing streams, with springs and underground waters welling up in valleys

7. Orlinsky, 27–64, especially 31–32.

and hills, a land of wheat and barley, of vines and fig trees and pomegran-
ates, a land of olive trees and honey, a land where you may eat bread without scarcity, where you will lack nothing, a land whose stones are iron and
from whose hills you may mine copper. You shall eat your fill and bless
the LORD your God for the good land that he has given you.

The expression "good land" frames this description of the territory
that Israel is to enjoy. The generous owner of all lands is providing the
Israelites with a choice site where they will have all the necessities of
life: an ample water supply, a rich variety of foods, and sufficient iron
and copper to make implements. The hyperbole of this lyrical propaganda emphasizes that Israel "will lack nothing." The land provided by
the celestial ruler is expected to make the Israelite vassals totally self-
sufficient.

This rhetoric emphasizes the indebtedness of the audience to the generous landowner who has given them a home, a territory of their own.
The Israelites are reminded, however, that this territory boasts the rem-
nants of a prior culture. Israel inherits "a land with fine, large cities that
you did not build, houses filled with all sorts of goods that you did not
fill, hewn cisterns that you did not hew, vineyards and olive groves that
you did not plant" (Deut. 6:10-11).

As Mark O'Brien has rightly pointed out, the polity of Deuteronomy
is concerned especially with how the Israelites will handle life in the
towns of this prior culture.[8] The incoming Israelites are portrayed as
vulnerable and inexperienced in urban life. In spite of the good, well-
provisioned homes and fertile gardens that Israel inherits from the
Canaanites, neither the indigenous peoples of the land nor their culture
is given any serious recognition in the ideology of this text.

What is especially good about Canaan as a land grant is the physical
domain for which YHWH, as the one ruling over the land and its fertility, can be given credit. The cult, customs, and polity of the Canaanite
peoples are all rejected as alien to the new order to be introduced by
YHWH. Because the ruler of all the earth has chosen Israel out of all the
peoples of the earth, Israel's cult, customs, and polity must be quite distinct. No exchange of cultural ideas is to be tolerated. The Canaanites

8. Mark O'Brien, "Authority in Israel: The Deuteronomic Contribution in Deut. 16:18—
18:22," International SBL Conference Paper, 1992; cf. Clements, *Deuteronomy,* chapter
7.

and their religious culture are worthless; in fact, the polity of the prior inhabitants is to be viewed as evil (Deut. 7:1-6, 25-26).

Although the Israelites did nothing to earn or develop this land, when they take possession of it, they will lack nothing.[9] They will owe everything to the owner of all lands who has contracted to give them this particular land as a unique act of divine largesse. Accordingly, this people should never forget their celestial benefactor or the oppressive land of Egypt from which YHWH rescued them (Deut. 6:12).

In the wilderness, a powerful memory of Egypt—with its fish, cucumbers, melons, and leeks—is of a land with satisfying foods. In contrast to Canaan, the land flowing with milk and honey (Deut. 6:3; 11:9), Egypt is the land where you sow your seed and irrigate by foot as one would a vegetable garden (11:10). Egypt, however, was also a land of slavery, even if it was a land of rich foods. Canaan is the good land because it is the territory where the Israelites will learn dependency on their liberator and landowner. The good land is a gift from this magnanimous landowner, an allocated territory to which Israel is given title.

THE LAND TREATY

As the owner of many lands, YHWH claims rulership over the conquered land of Canaan. The form and acknowledgment of YHWH's rule are expressed in a covenant or treaty that claims to be a continuation with the covenant established at Horeb (Deut. 5:2-3). Like the earthly rulers of great empires, YHWH establishes the conditions of allegiance and service for the people in the new land. The difference here is that Israel is not depicted as a vanquished people but as a relocated community of former slaves, and the land is not merely another conquered territory but a place chosen for YHWH's personally designed polity to be introduced.

If YHWH's claim to ownership over this land is to be credible, then the proposed treaty with Israel and its corresponding polity must succeed. YHWH, it seems, has a vested interest in the treaty that gives Israel conditional title to the land of Canaan. YHWH's style of rule and recommended polity are to be revealed to other lands through public

9. Brueggemann, *The Land*, 49–50.

actions in Israel. The experiment of a new polity under YHWH is to begin with Israel.

Israel's indebtedness to YHWH, the mighty and magnanimous landowner, is to provide the motivation for accepting the conditions necessary for residence in the allocated land. These conditions relate both to the success of Israel's initial occupation of the land (Deut. 4:1; 6:18) and to the possibility of living long on the land (5:33; 11:8-9), or even "for all time" (4:40). Israel's retention of the allotted territory of Canaan is conditional on keeping the stipulations of the landowner as articulated in the new polity for the land.

The covenant exhortations in Deuteronomy 4–9 speak of these stipulations explicitly as statutes (*ḥuqqim*) and ordinances (*mišpaṭim*). Whether or not these terms refer specifically to "constitutional matters," as McBride suggests,[10] they are clearly the particular stipulations to which Moses declares Israel to be bound by treaty (*berit*) in Deuteronomy 5:1-3. As the opening line of Deuteronomy 12:1 seems to indicate, these matters of polity about life in the territory of Canaan are those outlined in the law code of Deuteronomy 12:2—26:15. They are the *lex terrae.*

The formal ratification of this treaty or covenant, which obliges Israel to "observe these statutes and ordinances," immediately follows this law code (Deut. 26:16; cf. 4:5, 14). The public declaration of a ceremony announced in Deuteronomy 26:16-19 seals the Horeb covenant for the generation to whom Moses speaks. The subsequent blessings and curses (27–28) are typical of ancient Near Eastern treaties.[11]

As Andrew Hill has demonstrated, the Ebal ceremony (Deut. 27) reflects the elements of a land grant ceremony within the wider treaty structure.[12] The stones, the land gift, the witnesses, and the curses are all typical of grants that give legal title to new occupants of land. The landless Levites are instructed to recite the ceremony to the tribes who are expected to witness their grants. Retaining these grants, however, is conditional on keeping the law of the land (*lex terrae*) written on the stones marking the grant.

10. McBride, "Polity," 233–34.
11. See, for example, Dennis McCarthy, *Treaty and Covenant* (Rome: Biblical Institute Press, 1978).
12. Andrew Hill, "The Ebal Ceremony as Hebrew Land Grant?" *JETS* 31 (1988): 399–406.

What concerns us here is to explicate the way in which the territory of Canaan is allocated to the Israelites on condition that they remain faithful to these treaty stipulations that cannot be modified (Deut. 4:2-4). A prime stipulation of the treaty is that Israel refrain from making idols of anything on the land or in the sky (4:15-31). Moses himself takes a treaty oath to emphasize that if the Israelites act corruptly by making idols they will lose the territory allocated to them: "I call heaven and earth to witness against you today that you will soon utterly perish from the land that you are crossing the Jordan to occupy; you will not live long on it, but will be utterly destroyed" (Deut. 4:26).

The creation of idols is anticipated when Israel becomes "complacent in the land" (Deut. 4:25). Making such idols is specifically termed "to forget the covenant" (4:23), the treaty Israel made with YHWH to occupy and retain the territory of Canaan (4:25-31). In this context the God who has chosen Israel as a people is the sole "God in heaven above and earth below" (4:39; author's translation), who has allotted heavenly bodies for all people to enjoy, and not to worship in the form of idols (4:19).

Related to this prohibition against idols is the stipulation that Israel refrain from worshiping other gods (Deut. 6:14; 7:4; 8:19; 11:16). The owner of all lands, who dispossessed the nations of Canaan and allocated the territory to Israel, will dispossess Israel if other gods are worshiped (8:20). The gods that seem to be the target of this regulation are the gods of Canaan (7:1-6).

As the existing gods of the territory, these deities might be assumed to have some authority or priority in the land. The treaty YHWH makes with the Israelites requires total allegiance to the landowner and the removal of any local fertility deities that might detract from their recognizing YHWH's authority and developing an attitude of total dependency on their benefactor for blessing, life, and fertility in the land.

The promotion of a theocratic polity under YHWH as a generous experiment with Israel demands that the program be free from external contamination. For this polity to be tested, any alternative ideals or additional deities from other cultures need to be excluded. Israel must therefore have no interaction with the peoples of Canaan, no covenants, no intermarriage, and, above all, no contact with their gods or worship life (Deut. 7:1-6). For the polity of the land to work, it needs to be isolated from outside influence and singular in its focus.

These conditions and stipulations within the proposed polity for the land make it clear that the land is secondary and allegiance to YHWH is primary. The land is the domain chosen for an experimental polity under YHWH: Any land could have been chosen. The determinative bond that Israel must recognize is not with the land but with YHWH as the ruler. Israel must learn absolute obedience to the treaty maker or lose the land grant. The treaty, not the territory, is primary (Deut. 4:40; 6:13-18; 8:11-20; 11:16).

Ultimately, the land itself is also a temptation, a potential source of power and sufficiency other than God (Deut. 8:11-20). Israel must keep its distance from the land, and its eyes on the landowner;[13] otherwise, the Israelites will be tempted to exalt themselves (8:14), take the credit for prosperity in the land, and forget that they owe everything to YHWH.

The ruler of the earth relates to this territory in a particular way that underscores the land's dependency on YHWH as landowner. As maker of the treaty, YHWH is also committed to oversee the territory under treaty where this polity is to be established. From heaven the "eyes of the LORD" are continuously on the land, a land that YHWH specifically "cares for" (*daraš*, Deut. 11:12 RSV) with water from above (11:11-17).[14] It is from this habitation in heaven rather than on the land that YHWH blesses land and people (26:15).

Faithfulness to the treaty ensures that YHWH will send down "rain for your land in its season, the early rain and the later rain" (Deut. 11:14). Unfaithfulness leads to God shutting up the heavens "so that there will be no rain and the land will yield no fruit" (11:17). The treaty maker is the celestial rain-giver who opens rich storehouses in heaven and blesses the land with fertility (28:8-12). YHWH, not Baal, is the source of the land's fertility, a fertility that derives from God above, not from the earth or any gods below.

In the rhetoric of the ideology presented in Deuteronomy 4–11, there is no indication that the land of Canaan is God's own place, the locus of

---

13. Brueggemann, *The Land*, 53–59, depicts the land as a temptation.
14. John G. McConville, "1 Chronicles 28:9: Yahweh 'Seeks Out' Solomon," *JTS* 37 (1986): 105–8.

a special divine presence, as in the Abraham narratives. Israel is indeed the chosen people located by God in the territory of Canaan. It is a territory, however, from which God can remove Israel, in the same way that the Canaanites were removed (Deut. 4:26, 38; 8:20). YHWH's attachment and affinity are with the people rather than the place (4:25-31). YHWH's investment is in the treaty with Israel rather than in the land as a cherished abode. YHWH has no eternal kinship or bond with Canaan as a sacred land.

Consistent with this ideology is the so-called name theology of Deuteronomy. It is the name rather than the face (*panim*) or any visible representation of YHWH that is located at a chosen place in Canaan (Deut. 12:5, 11; 14:23; 16:6, 11; 26:2). YHWH keeps at a distance from the land. As ruler of heaven and earth, YHWH is not to be linked closely with the land. The name alone, which is the symbol of YHWH's authority, is the means of access to YHWH in the land.

YHWH claims to be the ruler of all lands, the God of heaven, who functions as a celestial overseer monitoring the territories of earth. With Israel YHWH has a special treaty that could ensure continuous occupation of the territory of Canaan. "All the peoples of the earth" will see the blessing of Israel if the people are faithful to their God (Deut. 28:1-10; 29:24-28).

THE LEVITES AND THE LAND

Discernment of the ideal social model for the land envisaged in the speeches of Moses is a complex exercise. The figure of Moses is clearly the hero of the narrative, and most of the text is represented as a report of his speeches. Moses, as the only one who received the constitutional law directly from God, gives authority to the power structures for urban living in this new land. Admittedly, Moses himself ends his career in disfavor and must hand over the occupation of the land to Joshua (Deut. 1:37-38; 3:23-28), but the law and treaty he represents persist in the polity of the land.

The structure that, according to the text of Deuteronomy, Moses established in the wilderness incorporates a simple organization of tribal groups with wise leaders (*ra'šim*) to enable the people and judges (*šopeṭim*) to administer justice fairly to all from the least to the greatest (Deut. 1:13-18). Elders (*zeqenim*), too, are remembered as leaders among the people, but their role is not clarified (5:23). Moses, however, remains the divinely appointed authority over all tribes, the final arbiter in all matters of justice and the sole source of theocratic law (1:15-17; 4:1, 5, 44; 5:31-32).

Who is to assume the continuing mantle of authority in the promised land? Whose interest is being served by promoting an ideology of total indebtedness to God for the land, a total negation of all the indigenous peoples of the land along with their religious culture, and a relentless demand to recognize Israel's absolute dependency on God as celestial ruler and sole source of blessing?

Even though Joshua is depicted as having the responsibility for conquering the land (Deut. 1:38), his descendants do not become the powerbrokers. Nor are the sons of Moses invested with authority. The figure of Aaron and presumably the priesthood that claimed Aaron as its eponymous ancestor lose credibility when the narrator has Moses include the story of the golden calf in his speech. It is only Moses' powerful role as mediator that rescues Aaron from God's fierce anger (9:15-21). In the law code, Aaron's descendants do not appear to be given any privileged status before God (cf. Num. 25:10-13) and are presumably included with all the Levites.

At the point where the ark of the covenant is introduced in Deuteronomy, the Levites are identified as the one group in Israel that has a unique and powerful status (Deut. 10:1-9).[15] Regardless of what groups were part of the faction that promoted the so-called Deuteronomic reform historically,[16] the text, as an ideological document, focuses on the Levites as those who ought to be the true leaders of Israel, the one group as a whole against whom YHWH has apparently not directed any anger.

15. In the extended debate about the relationship between priests and Levites, I would tend to agree with R. K. Duke, "The Portion of the Levite: Another Reading of Deuteronomy 18:6-8," *JBL* 106 (1987): 193–201, who makes it clear that all Levites are not necessarily priests in Deuteronomy. The status of the Levites promoted in Deuteronomy, be they priests or not, is not derived from being priests but from their role as guardians and interpreters of the law. Cf. John G. McConville, *Law and Theology in Deuteronomy* (Sheffield: JSOT Press, 1984). Baruch Halpern, "The Centralisation Formula in Deuteronomy," *VT* 31 (1981): 37, argues that "the deuteronomic code would enforce a hierarchical priestly monopoly on the cultic status quo."
16. P. Dutcher-Walls, "The Social Location of the Deuteronomists," *JSOT* 52 (1991): 77–94.

The threefold function of the Levites is specified as carrying the ark, standing before YHWH to minister, and blessing in YHWH's name (Deut. 10:8). The Levites thereby have access to God's presence and serve as guardians of the ark or, more specifically, the ten words of God that are deposited in the ark and that epitomize the constitutional law for the land.

It is the narrator, however, rather than Moses, who introduces the reader to the Levites.[17] The authority of the Levites, it seems, is not mediated through Moses but received directly from God: "At that time the LORD set apart the tribe of Levi" (Deut. 10:8). The privileged status of the tribe of Levi is further emphasized by the claim that "YHWH is his entitlement" (*nahalah,* 10:9; author's translation). Unlike other tribes who received land as their allotted entitlement, the Levites receive a higher portion. Further, this privileged status is based on a divine promise similar to that relating to the land itself (cf. 18:1-2). By contrast, Levites in other law codes are granted land around their towns to pasture animals (Num. 35:1-5).

The Levites' privileged position, introduced in Deuteronomy 10:8-9, serves as the charter for their role in the land. Subsequent references in the constitutional law itself outline how the people are to recognize the status of the Levites by providing them with the necessities of life (Deut. 12:11-12; 14:27-29; 18:1-8; 26:11-12). In these passages the Levites are grouped with male and female slaves, aliens, widows, and orphans, as though the Levites were among the disenfranchised or underprivileged of society. The common denominator among these groups is their landless status. The Levites, however, seem to be depicted as the landless elite claiming power over the landed; the other groups are all landless poor whom God expects to be remembered with similar acts of goodwill.

Once the entire book of the law is committed to writing, it is the Levites who place it beside the ark of the covenant, where it is to remain as a witness (Deut. 31:25-26). The Levites are clearly depicted as the guardians of the constitutional law and the land treaty articulated in Deuteronomy (17:14-20). It is the Levites, and especially the Levitical priests, who stand to gain by implementing the ideology of Deuteronomy.

17. R. Polzin, *Moses and the Deuteronomist* (New York: Seabury, 1980).

The authority of the Levites is emphasized further within the constitutional laws. The Levites minister before YHWH at the central shrine (Deut. 18:6-7); in matters of judicial dispute the Levitical priests assume the role of arbiter once played by Moses (21:5); any monarch who arises in the land must come to the Levitical priests to receive the law of the land over which the Levites are guardians (17:18); in matters of purity it is the Levitical priests who provide advice (24:8). Disobedience to any ruling on the law by judges or Levitical priests carries the death penalty (17:9-13).

The law of the covenant is the law of the land treaty, which the Israelites must keep if they are to maintain their tenancy in the land. The Levites claim authority over this law (cf. Deut. 33:10). They have no vested interests in owning land for themselves. Their power lies in the claim that if the Israelite landholders wish to retain their land they must heed the Levites and recognize their status. The Levites apparently claim to be the divinely ordained heirs of Moses, and the true rulers of an envisaged theocracy for the land and especially its towns. Retention of, or return to, the land demands a full recognition of the Levites as God's representatives in the land.

LAND RIGHTS AND JUSTICE

The ideology of the land as a grant supports the rights of the invading people to occupy the land by divine sanction. A divine promise to Israel's ancestors, a divine demonstration of conquering might, and a divine gift of the good land—all confirm Israel's entitlement to the land. This right, however, is conditional. Israel must obey the laws of the proposed polity for the land or face losing the land.

These land rights are grounded not in some ancient or sacred affinity with the land but in a treaty that prescribes the conditions for holding the land. The Israelites have no natural right to the land, only a promise of tenure if they are a faithful vassal people. Canaan is territory under treaty; the land grant is conditional.

By contrast, the rights of the original Canaanite inhabitants are totally dismissed and their culture negated. They are supposed to be exterminated.[18] This ideology ignores the historical reality that much of

18. Clements, *Deuteronomy*, 8, describes Deuteronomy 7:2 as "the most forthright demand for racial genocide that is to be found anywhere in the Old Testament."

Canaan's culture persisted in Israel and that many of the indigenous people of Canaan became part of the Israelite nation. The vision in Deuteronomy is of a nation purged by trials in the wilderness[19] and uncontaminated by the ways—and ideally by any presence—of the indigenous peoples of the land. The Canaanites have no rights to land and apparently no right to justice.

The elevation of the Levites to a position of power, in spite of their landless status, suggests that ultimately there is a higher concern than entitlement to land in Deuteronomy. The Levites have YHWH rather than the land as their entitlement (*nahalah*). This special entitlement gives the Levites power and status.

There are those in the ideal Deuteronomic society, however, who have neither land nor status. Any Canaanites who happen to survive the wars of YHWH are destined to survive as slave labor with no obvious rights to power or property (Deut. 21:10-11). Women captured in the war may be taken as wives and then dismissed if not suitable. Although they are not supposed to become slaves, they are nevertheless dishonored women with no standing or property (21:10-14).

Peasant landholders have entitlement to their individual properties by virtue of a divine allocation in the distant past. This allocation is explicitly designated a *nahalah*, a separate divine entitlement within the land as YHWH's grant to Israel (19:14). The family *nahalah* is a discrete portion of the total land as Israel's *nahalah*.

To protect the rights of the family to its entitlement, the Israelite ancestors set up boundary stones to mark borders of the property. In the land grant ceremony at Mount Ebal, a curse is invoked on any who dare to remove these boundary markers (Deut. 27:17; cf. Prov. 22:28). These laws enshrine the right of the ancestral families of Israel to property they believed to belong to them under an ancient divine land grant. No redistribution of the land to the landless in society is ever envisaged.

These landholders, however, are expected to take care of the needs of the landless who have no land rights. A portion of the harvest is to be left for the widows, orphans, and aliens (Deut. 24:19-20). The poor and the landless laborers are to be paid wages (24:14). Those without land rights are expected to find justice in the gates (24:7-10); Israelites are to

---

19. Van Seters, *Prologue to History*, chapter 13, highlights the significance of the wilderness experience as a preparation for possession of the land.

remember that they, too, were once landless slaves. If the judges of the community do not decide justly in such cases, Israel will lose the land (16:18-20).

This justice for the landless clearly means that those without power and property should not be exploited. There is no principle at work, however, that suggests that the landless, being Israelites within the land given as a *nahalah*, should themselves have a family or a personal land entitlement. Ultimately, in spite of the blessings of YHWH that should produce a society free of poor and presumably landless families (Deut. 15:4), the reality is that there will always be "poor in the midst of the land" (15:11; author's translation). This means that Israelite families with land and wealth are to show concern for a range of groups in society who are landless or destitute. These include slaves, debt slaves, servants, and laborers (15:7-18).

Clearly those families with traditional land entitlements have both status and responsibility in the land. Those without land entitlements are dependent on the goodwill of the landed. Justice in this context does not mean the redistribution of land but rather preventing exploitation of the landless.[20] At the same time, this expression of justice within existing structures of the Deuteronomic polity means that the landless poor are made dependent on the landed peasants and elite for survival and security.

SUMMARY

The ideology of the book of Deuteronomy promotes a theocracy in which YHWH has conquered the land for Israel's occupation, demands all the credit for these achievements, and expects a corresponding sense of total indebtedness on Israel's part. The image of the land as good and prosperous is designed to heighten Israel's sense of total gratitude. All the good things of the good land are derived from YHWH.

The process of YHWH "giving" (*ntn*) the land to Israel makes Canaan a divinely sanctioned and legal land grant.

---

20. Contrary to the claim of Gunther Wittenberg, "The Significance of Land in the Old Testament," *Journal for Theology in South Africa* 77 (1991): 58–60, I see no explicit evidence that the Deuteronomic law is designed to enable the poor to regain the land. When debt slaves are released, they are to be given goods, but no mention is made of land.

The central symbol of the land as a grant from YHWH functions in three different ways in this ideology. First, it reinforces the indebtedness of Israel to YHWH. Second, it is promoted as the charter of Israel's rightful entitlement to the land. Third, it serves to justify the dispossession of the original inhabitants of the land and negate their rights.

None of the gods, customs, or polity of the conquered inhabitants are to be recognized as valuable. YHWH, whose abode is in heaven, chooses the land of Canaan as the locus for an experimental relationship with a newly chosen people. It is YHWH's affinity for this people, rather than for the land, that is primary.

A treaty or covenant, reflecting this special relationship, is established between the Israelites and their landowner, YHWH. Survival in the land is conditional on faithfulness to this treaty. This treaty outlines a polity with laws and procedures that must be obeyed if life is to prosper on the land under YHWH as celestial ruler. Violation of this treaty can mean removal or extermination from the land. The laws of this treaty are the *lex terrae*.

Power in the theocracy of Deuteronomy is located with the Levites as the guardians of the *lex terrae*. Peasants from ancestral families have the right to their traditional lands. The poor, aliens, and the Canaanites have no right to own land.

CHAPTER 4

Land as Family Lots:
An Ancestral Household
Ideology

In the famous *Heilsgeschichte* theology of Gerhard von Rad, the book of Joshua is viewed as part of a Hexateuch and linked structurally with the preceding books and traditions of the Pentateuch. Von Rad bases his thesis on the fact that, in the ancient credos of Israel, "the granting of the land was the last of the saving acts of Jahweh."[1] Given this orientation, the book of Joshua is a narrative text designed to reflect the theological fulfillment of promises of land made to the Israelite ancestors.

A second major approach is to view the book of Joshua as part of a grand theological introduction to the so-called Deuteronomistic history of Israel stretching from the books of Deuteronomy or Joshua through Kings.[2] YHWH's promise and conquest of Canaan for "all Israel" are viewed as the first era in the theological history of Israel.

Clearly there are points of continuity between the themes of the book of Joshua and the Pentateuch, just as there are connections with the subsequent portraits of the history of Israel. Such connections, however, ought not deny the book of Joshua a voice of its own. In this chapter, therefore, we consider Joshua as a discrete literary product[3] with a dis-

---

1. Gerhard von Rad, *Old Testament Theology,* Vol. 1 (Edinburgh: Oliver & Boyd, 1962), 297.
2. Mark O'Brien, "The 'Deuteronomistic History' as a Story of Israel's Leaders," *Australian Biblical Review* 37 (1989): 14–34; Peter Diepold, *Israel's Land* (Stuttgart: Kohlhammer, 1972).
3. The literary character of Joshua is explored by writers such as David M. Gunn, "Joshua and Judges," in *The Literary Guide to the Bible,* edited by Robert Alter and Frank Kermode (Cambridge: Harvard University, Belknap Press, 1987), 102–21; and L. Daniel Hawk, *Every Promise Fulfilled: Contesting Plots in Joshua* (Louisville: Westminster/John Knox, 1991).

tinct theological and ideological force, taking the account of the division of the land as pivotal for understanding the land ideology of the book.

Significant also is a recognition of the social and political forces involved in creating the ideology of the book of Joshua.[4] According to Keith Whitelam, for example,

> The projection of their current situation in the past, couched in terms of a divine promise, legitimises their right to return and claim the land that has been occupied by those who either did not face deportation or have later moved into the area in the intervening period. The conquest traditions in Joshua and Judges provide an explicit legitimisation of the returnees' right to the land. The narratives continually emphasise the rights of "Israel" entering from outside to take possession (*yrš*) of the land and in particular to dispossess (*yrš*) those groups already in the land (Josh. 13ff.; Judg. 1). There is an underlying theme of antagonism between the occupants of the land and the true "Israel" who are being led from captivity to occupy that very land.[5]

Whitelam and others argue that the book of Joshua provides an ideological basis for those in exile returning to take possession of their land, whereas the book of Chronicles represents the claim of those who did not go into exile and are still in possession of part of the land. Although Whitelam's position is plausible, the precise political context that shaped Joshua may be disputed. There is little doubt, however, that the book promotes an ideological charter for claiming possession of the land.

Our task here is to explore the central features of that ideology, taking into account the central image of land allotment, the character of YHWH as owner of the land, the function of the conquest narratives, the role of Joshua as land-giver, the concept of power located in the ancestral household, and themes of rights and resistance in the conquest narrative.

---

4. Our study is not concerned with the recent research into the social and political forces involved in the historical emergence of Israel as a people, hints of which may be reflected in the text of Joshua. Some of the key works in this research include Norman Gottwald, *The Tribes of Yahweh;* Robert Coote, *Early Israel;* and Thomas Thompson, *Early History of the Israelite People: From the Written and Archaeological Sources* (Leiden: E. J. Brill, 1992). Our interest here is in the ideology of the present text about the Israelites and their land, not the origins of Israel as a political entity.

5. Keith Whitelam, "Israel's Traditions of Origin: Reclaiming the Land," *JSOT* 44 (1989): 30.

In this chapter *ancestral household* refers to the *bet ʾab*, the smallest socioeconomic unit in Israel, involving several generations of family under a single head, a cluster of dwellings forming a single household, and a range of economic activities.[6] This unit is to be distinguished from the ancestral family (*mišpeḥah*), which, as Norman Gottwald shows, refers to a protective association of ancestral families or households (cf. Josh. 7:14).[7]

LAND ALLOTMENT

Central to the ideology of the book of Joshua is the image of the land as a cluster of family lots or allotments. The divine process of granting (*ntn*) the land culminates in the act of dividing (*ḥlq*) the land into identifiable lots with recognizable boundaries. These lots are assigned to the ancestral families (*mišpeḥot*) of the tribes of Israel at various locations within Canaan, including the Transjordanian territories.[8]

The allotment for each cluster of tribal families is designated its *goral* or "lot" (Josh. 15:1; 16:1; 17:1; 18:11; 19:1; etc.), a term that initially reflects the action of casting lots to determine the divinely approved allocation, but that later comes to mean allotted land or estate.[9] The

6. Raymond Westbrook, *Property and Family in Biblical Law* (Sheffield: JSOT Press, 1991), 12–14; L. E. Stager, "The Archeology of the Family in Ancient Israel," *BASOR* 260 (1985): 18–23; Carol Meyers, " 'To Her Mother's House': Considering a Counterpart to the Israelite *bet ʾab*," in *The Bible and the Politics of Exegesis*, edited by David Jobling et al. (Cleveland: Pilgrim, 1992), 39–51. Meyers, 41, renders *bet ʾab* as "family household." Although this expression captures the multigenerational character and the diverse functions of this social group, it loses the link with the "father" or "ancestor" with whom the family line is associated. I have chosen to follow Shmuel Ahituv, "Land and Justice," in *Justice and Righteousness,* edited by Henning Graf Reventlow and Yair Hoffman (Sheffield: JSOT Press, 1992), 11–28, and others who render the expression "ancestral household."
7. Gottwald, *The Tribes of Yahweh,* 315–17; see also Meyers, " 'To Her Mother's House,' " 39.
8. Ahituv identifies the differences between the Joshua and Numbers (Num. 26) accounts of land distribution. Unlike the account in Joshua, the Numbers account attempts to follow a principle of equal distribution according to the numbers in each tribe identified in a census.
9. Ahituv, 18. A. G. Auld, *Joshua, Moses and the Land* (Edinburgh: Clark, 1980), chapter 4, following a tradition-critical approach and the text of the LXX, which reads *gebul* for *goral* in several places, argues that the references specifically to lot (*goral*) are later additions. The priority of the LXX text at this point is debatable. In any case, Joshua is portrayed as allotting pieces of land to each ancestral family, but lots are just one of the modes of allocation. Clearly the final form of the Joshua text promotes the image of the land as a cluster of lots.

"entitlement" of each ancestral family is explicitly identified "by lot, as the LORD has commanded Moses" (14:2; cf. 19:51; Num. 26:53-56). Thus the distribution of the land by lot is promoted in this ideology as being by divine command with authority from Moses and through the agency of Joshua (Josh. 11:23; 23:4).

The lot of each tribe and extended family is explicitly identified as its divine entitlement (*nahalah*, Josh. 14:2).[10] Although the whole land of Canaan may viewed as an entitlement (*nahalah*) for Israel as a people (11:23), this entitlement is explicitly "according to its ancestral families" (13:15, 24, 29; 15:1, 20; 16:5; author's translation); the land is a cluster of family lots granted as "entitlements" (11:23; 19:49, 51; 24:28; author's translation). In the book of Joshua, land entitlement is specific to tribe and ancestral family according to a schema that presents a utopian image of the past.

Each entitlement, given by divine lot according to the command of Moses, apparently becomes the inheritance of its ancestral family and household in subsequent generations. Thus the ideology of the book of Joshua provides a charter for ancestral households to claim these inherited lands as territory given by divine decree, regardless of what may have happened to the ownership of these lands over time.[11] The allotment narratives in the book of Joshua are a sacral justification for these claims.

In the text, the land of Canaan is explicitly identified as a cluster of royal lands to be distributed by Joshua. When Joshua conquers Canaan, he is said to have taken the monarchs "and their land" (Josh. 10:42). It is specifically "their land" that is allotted to the tribes of Israel (12:7). In this land ideology, the ordinary families of Israel receive the royal lands of Canaan as their entitlements. In the distribution, the royal lands of Canaan are transformed into a land of family lots.[12]

---

10. On the meaning and rendering of *nahalah*, see the excursus on *nahalah* following chapter 2.

11. The import of this warning would not be lost on later Israelite families who no longer have possession of their ancestral lands, for whatever reason. Such reasons may include appropriation of lands by the monarch, sale of land to pay for debts, or acquisition by foreigners during the exile.

12. The antiroyal thrust of the text of the book of Joshua is a reflection of its ideology when the text became a literary product, rather than evidence of a peasant revolt against Canaanite oppression in the early history of Israel, as Gottwald proposes in *The Tribes of Yahweh*, 210–19, 498–554.

The narrative of land distribution presents a number of significant variations in the mode of land division. The allotment to the tribes of the Transjordan is remembered as the work of Moses himself on the plains of Moab (Josh. 13:8, 15, 24, 29, 32). The allotment at Gilgal begins with a case of special pleading. Accompanied by the people of Judah, Caleb reminds Joshua of Caleb's bravery in an earlier attempt to enter Canaan and the promise of Moses that Caleb would have an entitlement that lasts forever (14:9, 14). Gilgal is presumably also the site for the casting of lots to determine the allocations of Judah, Ephraim, and half of Mannaseh (15–17).

Two other cases of special pleading are recorded among these allocations. The first involves Caleb promising his daughter Achsah to the warrior who captures the town of Kiriath-sepher. After this is accomplished, Caleb invites his daughter to state her wish. Achsah responds by requesting that Caleb give (*ntn*) her springs of water in the Negeb where she is to be located (Josh. 15:16-19).

The second account of special pleading concerns the five daughters of Zelophehad who obtain entitlement in the land because Zelophehad has no sons to carry on the family line (Josh. 17:3-6). Land allotment is therefore not depicted as a uniform and automatic process; according to the text, Caleb, Achsah, Joshua, the Levites, the daughters of Zelophehad, and the house of Joseph are associated with special requests in relation to their allotments.

These examples illustrate that the ideology of the land allocation applauds individual initiative in claiming land. These assertive groups do not wait for a total dispossession and distribution of the land under Joshua or some other authorized leader. Rather, they take the independent action necessary to take actual possession of their individual claims.

The remaining seven tribes receive their land entitlement when Israel assembles at Shiloh (Josh. 18:1). The land allotment process on this occasion is preceded by an official land survey in which the remaining territories are divided into portions, described formally in writing. This process produces a land survey document, which is officially designated a book (*seper*, 18:9). Thus the claim of these extended families to areas of land is grounded in the tradition of a sacred text of title deeds. Joshua is then portrayed as casting lots before YHWH to determine which of the seven tribes God has chosen for each of the particular allotments (cf. Mic. 2:5).

Still another method of allotment is employed in relation to the cities of refuge. In this narrative, YHWH takes the initiative and commands Joshua to tell the Israelites to set apart specified cities as "a refuge from the avenger of blood" (Josh. 20:1-3). These cities are a means by which YHWH can play a role as the protector of justice in the case of unintentional manslaughter.

The special allotments for the Levites are explicitly requested by the heads of their ancestral households (Josh. 21:1). These consist of towns with adjoining pasture lands for livestock (21:3, 4, 41-42). Thus the lots for the Levite families, including the house of Aaron, are interspersed among the family lots of the other tribes of Israel.

Joshua, as the faithful leader of the invading Israelites, is singled out for separate consideration at the end of the process and is given a town for his own household as a special entitlement. In this case, too, Joshua takes the initiative and requests a town, which Israel allocates as his entitlement. At the end of the book, Joshua is buried in his entitlement as Sarah and Abraham are buried in the lot purchased by the head of the first ancestral household.

YHWH, OWNER OF THE LAND

In the ideology of the book of Joshua, YHWH is the owner of the land who invites the families of Israel to possess the land they have been allocated. The land of Canaan is "YHWH's land" (Josh. 22:19; author's translation), and those who have a "portion in the LORD" enjoy a place in YHWH's land (22:25). YHWH carefully guides the allocation of each portion of the land by divine lot. This action legitimates the claims of future Israelite families to particular allotments of YHWH's land.

The extent of YHWH's own land promised to Israel seems to correspond to the territories that YHWH allocates to the designated families of Israel; YHWH's land is the cluster of family lots to which ancestral families can lay claim. In the opening speech to Joshua, however, YHWH reports that Moses was once promised a much more extensive domain (Josh. 1:4), reaching to Lebanon and the River Euphrates and incorporating all the land of the Hittites. The lands promised to Israel, therefore, are depicted as greater than the land of Canaan, as represented by the lands conquered and allocated as Israel's home.

YHWH is depicted as a terrifying ally, ready to fight the foes of Israel and dispossess those who hold the land that is to be allocated to chosen families (Josh. 13:6, 23; 10:13). YHWH's capacity as a warrior deity is illustrated in the way Joshua wins battles in the early conquest campaigns (Josh. 6 and 10). YHWH is depicted as a frightening deity employing mighty celestial forces. YHWH hails massive stones down "from heaven" (10:11) and halts the sun in the sky to win a total victory (10:12-14). This portrayal of YHWH in military mode reflects an ideology of terror typical of conquest narratives.[13]

YHWH is repeatedly remembered as a deity who has performed a catalog of heroic deeds; the feats of the Joshua campaign add to an already long list of heroics (Josh. 24:2-13). Even Canaanite harlots like Rahab know about the crossing of the Sea of Reeds and the victory over the two kings of the Amorites (2:10). The Gibeonites, too, have heard about events in Egypt and the fate of the two kings of the Amorites (9:9-10). Clearly, victory over these kings in the Transjordan is viewed as evidence that YHWH is already fulfilling the promise to dispossess the land and seen as evidence of the political ascendancy of a deity who claims to own the land and have authority to dispossess the indigenous peoples of the land.

In line with the ideology of divine ownership, it is YHWH, not Israel, who destroys Israel's foes and clears YHWH's land. YHWH reminds the Israelites "it was not by your sword or by your bow" that they obtained the land of Canaan (Josh. 24:12-13). YHWH is the all-sufficient warrior who dispossesses the land for the chosen people. The ideal of YHWH as the mysterious power able to guarantee victory provides the ideological impetus for those who, like Joshua, take the initiative to possess their allotted lands. The faithful are assured that YHWH will exhibit an array of celestial armory on their behalf. YHWH has the fire-

---

13. K. Lawson Younger, *Ancient Conquest Accounts*, 66, 233; cf. Jeffrey Niehaus, "Joshua and Ancient Near Eastern Warfare," *JETS* 31 (1988): 42; Moshe Weinfeld, "Divine Intervention in War in Ancient Israel and in the Ancient Near East," in *History, Historiography and Interpretation*, edited by Hayim Tadmore and Moshe Weinfeld (Jerusalem: Magnes Press, 1983), 121–47.

power to keep the promises made to Moses that the Israelites would possess the land of Canaan.

But, according to the text, Joshua, the model leader, makes it clear that this God is a "jealous God" (Josh. 24:19). YHWH tolerates no rival deities. If the Israelites serve any foreign gods, be they Canaanite or Egyptian, then YHWH "will turn and do you harm, and consume you, after doing you good" (24:20; author's translation). In YHWH's own land, YHWH demands unequivocal allegiance from all Israelite families. The jealousy of YHWH also extends to mixing and intermarriage with the survivors of the nations in the land (23:7, 12). Violation of this demand will mean that Israel will perish from the "good land that YHWH your God has given you" (23:13; author's translation).

In general, the various conquered peoples of Canaan are put under the ban (*herem*) and dedicated to YHWH; their total destruction is required (Josh. 6:21). YHWH expects Israel to show the Canaanites no mercy and accord them no rights. The terror ideology is relentless. Those Canaanites who survive do so by their own initiative and their total acknowledgment of YHWH as the God of the conquest. Rahab, Caleb, and the Gibeonites are viewed as Israelites in disguise. As the Gibeonites confess, "Your servants have come . . . because of the name of the LORD your God" (9:9).

Caleb the Kenizzite is an honorary Israelite. He is granted an allotment in YHWH's land as an exceptional case. He and the people of Judah come to plead the case of a Canaanite who has been more faithful to YHWH during the wilderness period than the people of Israel themselves (Josh. 14:6-14). He is a bold example of initiative, faithfulness, and courage for other households to follow.

The domain of YHWH is represented in the confession of Rahab as extending over earth and heaven (Josh. 2:11). The narrative has Joshua referring to YHWH as the "living God" who has the terrifying power to annihilate the various peoples of Canaan who live in YHWH's land (3:10). Joshua also announces that "the ark of the covenant of the God of all the land" will travel at the forefront of the march into Canaan (3:11; author's translation). "All the land" belongs to YHWH. YHWH's entry into this land is a spectacular ritual act as glorious as the crossing of the Sea of Reeds (3:14-17).

Thus the ideology of the book of Joshua presents a portrait of YHWH as the God of the land who promises total military support to any who press their divinely approved land claims in a spirit of total commitment to YHWH. YHWH led Joshua to glory; YHWH can do the same thing for any ancestral household or family who puts its total trust in YHWH's promise of land (cf. Josh. 23:10).

THE VISION AND REALITY OF CONQUEST

The stories of allotment and taking possession of allotments told in Joshua 13–21 are framed by conquest narratives (Josh. 1–12) and closing speeches ascribed to Joshua (23–24). Integral to that framing process are bold statements of the narrator that all YHWH's promises made to the ancestors had been kept as predicted by Moses (1:3-6). These fulfilled promises are said to include Joshua taking the whole land, the Israelites receiving their land entitlement, YHWH defeating all Israel's enemies within the land, and Israel enjoying rest from warfare (11:23; 21:43-45; 23:1).

Why does the narrator frame the text with these statements of fulfillment when the accounts themselves (e.g., Josh. 13:2-6, 13; 15:63; 16:10; 17:12-15; 18:2) and the speeches ascribed to Joshua clearly indicate that the problem for the implied audience is a land that has not really been possessed? Even if one assumes that the narrator is using earlier sources, the difficulty of this glaring discrepancy remains. Lyle Eslinger, following the lead of Robert Polzin, demonstrates that, from a literary perspective, the narrator's statements function as irony.[14] But how do such ironic statements—and, indeed, the opening stories of Israel's unified conquest of the land—promote the ideology of the book?

One might equivocate and contend that the Deuteronomic editor understood the taking of the land to mean gaining control without eliminating all the opposition.[15] K. Lawson Younger argues quite convincingly that references to a total conquest of the land are hyperbole typical

---

14. Lyle Eslinger, *Into the Hands of the Living God* (Sheffield: Almond, 1989), 31; Polzin.

15. Gordon Wenham, "The Deuteronomic Theology of the Book of Joshua," *JBL* 90 (1971): 140–48. Brevard Childs, *An Introduction to the Old Testament as Scripture* (Philadelphia: Fortress, 1979), 249, views the passages depicting a complete conquest in Joshua as "a unique theological perspective of the Deuteronomic editor."

of ancient conquest accounts and are not to be interpreted as the work of a theological redactor.[16] But what is the function of this hyperbole in the political program of the book?

As a mechanism for promoting the ideology of Joshua, it seems likely that the narrator is promoting a vision for the implied audience of the book to affirm. That vision is one of a God who has given Israel all the land, as promised to the ancestors. The book of Joshua is more than the glorified annals of a military campaign. The text of Joshua incorporates an ideology that upholds the truth of total conquest as the ground of faith and the impetus for action.

Thus the expansive formulation of that vision functions as a provocation for the Israelites to claim and possess the land that is theirs by divine allotment. YHWH has kept faith. It is incumbent on the people to do their part and possess the land. The Israelites are being summoned to make the vision a reality in their lives.

The speech of Joshua to the people assembled at Shiloh (Josh. 18:1) tends to confirm this argument. While the narrator, quite appropriately, states the orthodox position that "the land lay subdued" before Israel (18:1), the speech ascribed to Joshua includes a vehement castigation of seven tribes for not possessing the land: "How long will you be slack about going in and taking possession (yrš) of the land that YHWH, the God of your ancestors, has given you?" (Josh. 18:3; author's translation).

Joshua is depicted in prophetic mode, chiding Israel for laxity in claiming the land. The final task of taking possession has not been completed by the various Israelite families and ancestral households. It is no longer Joshua's role to possess the land. That task is now the responsibility of the individual tribes and families, who have apparently failed to take the necessary initiative to claim, conquer, and possess their lands.

Earlier in the book, the narrator comments that Joshua had himself been reminded by YHWH that "very much of the land still remains to be possessed" (Josh. 13:2). Joshua is commanded to allocate this land to the tribes according to their entitlement (13:6-7). This action means shifting the onus for taking possession of the land from Joshua to the families and tribes themselves. The propaganda of the book of Joshua seems designed to provoke the families of Israel to take over the land

16. Younger, *Ancient Conquest Accounts,* 243.

they have been allotted and to accept YHWH's promise to help them dispossess the inhabitants (13:6).

Perhaps the most pointed and ironic word of Joshua to the implied audience is his parting gift to the Israelites, "I have allotted to you as an entitlement (*nahalah*) for your tribes those nations that remain, along with all the nations which I have already cut off" (Josh. 23:4; author's translation).

What a gift! Entrenched enemy nations in your own land! Elsewhere the term *nahalah* refers to the promised land as Israel's entitlement (Josh. 11:23). Instead of bequeathing the land as Israel's entitlement, Joshua gives his people the enemy nations that still have to be conquered. Joshua leaves Israel, as it were, holding the bag. Joshua did his part in cutting off nations. Now Israelite families must do theirs and take the initiative needed to possess the land.

The land allotment narrative of Joshua, therefore, seems to promote an ideology that urges ancestral families to take the initiative and claim their lands. These lands, according to this tradition, were allotted by YHWH at the time of Joshua. Ancestral households and families are called to make the orthodox vision enunciated by the narrator a living reality in the land they have been allotted.

This ideological position is bolstered by recounting the success stories of those ancestral families who took the initiative at the time of Joshua. A prime example is that of Caleb. When he comes to claim the land promised him, he pleads his faithfulness to YHWH during the days of Israel's wilderness wanderings. He quotes an oath of Moses, saying, "Surely the land on which your foot has trodden shall be an entitlement (*nahalah*) for you and your children forever, because you have wholeheartedly followed YHWH, my God" (Josh. 14:9; author's translation).

Subsequently Caleb is allotted Hebron as his entitlement. The account records that he then took the initiative to drive out the giant Anakim from the city (Josh. 15:13-14). He subsequently allots springs to Achsah, his daughter, whose hand is won by the warrior conquering the town of Kiriath-sepher (15:16-19).

Caleb is depicted as a model of faithfulness, initiative, warrior skills, and generosity for Israelites of all time. This is all the more striking in view of the fact that Caleb is in fact a Kenizzite, and not one of the favored ancestral households of Israel. He alone, of all the groups requesting or gaining allotment, is blessed by Joshua and thereby guaranteed success (Josh. 14:13). Caleb clearly is the "favored one." The message of Caleb's example seems to be that if a committed non-Israelite can claim his heritage as an inalienable entitlement promised by Moses, surely the ancestral families of Israel could do the same.

The bold action of the daughters of Zelophehad in gaining entitlements for their ancestral household (Josh. 17:3-6) provides a further example of initiative that ought to inspire Israelite families to follow suit and acquire their allotted land. If Israelite daughters, dedicated to preserving the ancestral line, can press their claim for land, surely Israelite male warriors should do the same.

The request of the house of Joseph to obtain additional land allotments is argued on the grounds that YHWH has blessed them with great numbers (Josh. 17:14). Joshua grants the house of Joseph an additional lot with the understanding that it clear the forests and drive the Canaanite inhabitants out of the hill country (17:17-18). The acquisition of this land entitlement is to involve the ancestral families of Joseph in a new struggle. It is no longer the responsibility of Joshua, leading a unified Israelite army, to dispossess and settle the land allotted. Settlement is here the task of the strong household of Joseph having the courage and taking the initiative and action necessary.

The Danites, too, are singled out for their actions in land acquisition. In spite of losing their portion, they take up arms, take possession (*yrš*), and settle (*yšb*) Leshem, whose name is changed to Dan (Josh. 19:47-48). This action of recapturing allotted land, coming at the very end of the allotments, may again provide a message for the implied audience of the text: Go and do likewise. Dispossession here is no longer seen as the responsibility of Joshua.

JOSHUA, THE IDEAL LEADER

Joshua is presented as the model of leadership in the conquest and acquisition of land. In this capacity he exercises control over the various power groups of Israel. He gives directions not only to the army and to the representatives of the tribes but also to the priests who carried the ark (Josh. 3:6; 6:8; 8:3-4); it is Joshua who directs the priests to take the ark ahead of the Israelites as they cross the Jordan (3:6).

In connection with this event, the narrator claims YHWH specifically informs Joshua that his action of commanding the priests who bear the ark exalts Joshua to the same status as Moses (Josh. 3:7-8). Clearly, then, the power of the Levitical priests, so evident in Deuteronomy, is depicted in this ideology as less than that of Joshua and whomever Joshua represents. As George Coats remarks, "Joshua manipulates the Levites and the ark as a single instrument."[17] Joshua is the hero of the entry in his own right.

Joshua has long been recognized as a new Moses and a divinely authenticated successor to Moses (Josh. 1:3, 5, 17, 18; 3:7; 4:14).[18] There are many obvious parallels with Moses, not the least of which is the crossing of the Jordan in a mode reminiscent of the crossing of the Sea of Reeds (3:14-17). YHWH promises to be with Joshua as YHWH was with Moses (1:5), and the people promise to obey Joshua "just as we obeyed Moses" (1:17).

In one respect, however, Joshua outshines Moses. Joshua, unlike Moses, has been totally faithful to YHWH and is the one privileged leader from the wilderness days to enter and enjoy the promised land. He concludes the exodus-wilderness era and ushers in the conquest-possession era. He is the symbol of supreme courage from the past who is represented as making the promises of YHWH to Moses a reality.

The Joshua stories, from the opening Rahab narrative, are designed to hail Joshua as the hero to be followed.[19] Joshua's espionage tactics succeed in winning the support of the household of Rahab and tricking the king of Jericho. The spies escape their pursuers and report that even before any battles are waged the inhabitants are smitten with fear. In fact, YHWH has already "given all the land into our hands" (Josh. 2:24).

Tricking the king of Jericho signals the beginning of a long sequence of victories over kings. Monarchs are no match for Joshua and his God. "The kings of the Amorites beyond the Jordan to the west" and "the kings of the Canaanites by the sea" melt with fear when they hear about YHWH's deeds achieved through Joshua (Josh. 5:1). Joshua's God is

---

17. George Coats, "The Ark of the Covenant in Joshua: A Probe into the History of a Tradition," *Hebrew Annual Review* 9 (1985): 141.
18. Dennis McCarthy, "The Theology of Leadership in Joshua 1–9," *Biblica* 52 (1971): 175; Wenham, 145.
19. McCarthy, "The Theology of Leadership," 170.

the symbol of an ideology of terror typical of ancient Near Eastern conquest accounts.[20] With the terrifying conquest of Jericho, Joshua's fame spreads throughout the land (6:27). The king of Ai, too, collapses before Joshua's fierce onslaught.

Subsequently, coalitions of kings arise to oppose Joshua (Josh. 9:1-2; 10:1-5; 11:1-5). Joshua takes on these coalitions as a defensive action. The Canaanites, not Joshua, are depicted as the aggressors. They first "hear" about the deeds of Joshua and then unite against him.[21] Joshua is not depicted as a peasant leader revolting against oppressive rulers, but rather as the community leader coming to settle land given to the people by legitimate divine charter. As a result, he and his people are attacked by the monarchs ruling the cities in YHWH's land.

Is Joshua a model forerunner of David, Josiah, or an idealized Deuteronomic monarch, as some scholars would argue?[22] Is Joshua a premonarchical paradigm of an ideal ruler? The evidence of the text suggests few, if any, of the features typical of an ideal royal ideology. By the end of the book, Joshua has established no centralized court, temple, militia, or administration. Rather, he encourages each ancestral house, family, and tribe to claim and conquer its own lands. Joshua sends the people to their own entitlements and makes no provision for a successor. Joshua is no monarch.

The text also exhibits an antiroyal message in relation to the foreign monarchs. They cannot survive if the people of God are faithful to YHWH and follow the lead of a figure like Joshua or Caleb. The campaign narrative closes with a long roll call of fallen monarchs whose lands Joshua has taken (Josh. 12:7-24). The failure of monarchs to survive the Joshua campaign suggests an ideology that looks beyond monarchs to Israelite leaders like Joshua, Caleb, and the heads of ancestral households, who all take the initiative and possess their land.

20. Younger, *Ancient Conquest Accounts,* 233.

21. Lawson Stone, "Ethical and Apologetic Tendencies in the Redaction of the Book of Joshua," *Catholic Biblical Quarterly* 53 (1991): 25–35.

22. Ray Sutherland, "Israelite Political Theory in Joshua 9," *JSOT* 53 (1992): 71, follows R. Nelson, "Josiah in the Book of Joshua," *JBL* 100 (1981): 531–40, in arguing that Joshua is "an intentional prefigurement of both King Josiah and an idealized deuteronomic king." Magnus Ottosson, *Josuaboken: en Programskrift for Davidsk Restauration* (Stockholm: Almqvist & Wiksell, 1991), claims the book depicts Joshua as the perfect Israelite monarch, whose obedience to the law of Moses guarantees retention of the land and restoration of the Davidic empire.

Joshua is also viewed as having authority over the priests and heads of ancestral families in the allotment and settlement of the land. He has the capacity to summon all Israel, including elders, heads of families, judges, and officers, to one place (Josh. 23:2; 24:1). He is portrayed as the model leader who has the capacity to unify the Israelites in their struggle to claim the land but, unlike a typical monarch, takes only a small town as his allotted entitlement (19:49-50).

AN ANCESTRAL HOUSEHOLD IDEAL

Whose ideals are represented by this model of Joshua? In whose interests are Joshua's exemplary conquests and commitment being promoted? An answer to this question is suggested by a comment of John Van Seters: "Joshua 24, however, seems to envisage a different situation, and therefore a different conception of covenant. The challenge is made to the people no longer as one nation but as so many individual households who are called to follow Joshua's example."[23]

Van Seters views Joshua 24 as an independent literary work whose origin he locates in the exile. He rightly recognizes Joshua as a religious leader who leads from example. A close examination of the book of Joshua suggests that Joshua 24 can be viewed as the culmination of an interest throughout the book in the ancestral household (*bet 'ab*), with Joshua presented as the ideal leader of an Israelite household.

Joshua challenges the Israelites to follow his example: "as for me and my house, we will serve the LORD" (Josh. 24:15 RSV). He confronts other households with the example of his ancestral household rather than with a direct divine command or curse. Joshua's household is the model ancestral household (*bet 'ab*). The tables are turned. The time has come for Israelite households to actively "choose" (*bḥr*) YHWH rather than passively accept the tradition that YHWH has chosen (*bḥr*) them as a people (Deut. 7:6) and given them the land as their entitlement.[24]

At strategic points throughout Joshua, family households and/or the heads of households play important roles. The opening conquest narra-

---

23. John Van Seters, "Joshua 24 and the Problem of Tradition in the Old Testament," in *In the Shelter of Elyon: Essays on Ancient Palestinian Life and Literature*, edited by W. Barrick and J. Spencer (Sheffield: JSOT Press, 1984), 153.

24. William Koopmans, *Joshua 24 as Poetic Narrative* (Sheffield: JSOT Press, 1992), 429.

tive is an account of how spies enter the house of Rahab. Her confession of faith in YHWH as the God of the exodus and the conquest (Josh. 2:9-11) parallels that of Joshua at the end of the book (24:2-13). Her commitment, like that of Joshua, means that her ancestral household (*bet 'ab*) also survives (2:12-14). Thus the paradigm of two committed ancestral households, the one Canaanite and the other Israelite, frames the narratives of Joshua.

The survival of Rahab and her family is also emphasized in the narrative of the conquest of Jericho. She saves not only her immediate ancestral household (*bet 'ab*, Josh. 6:17, 25) but also her ancestral family (*mišpeḥah*, 6:23). Just as the family of Rahab, a Canaanite, is saved by her faithfulness, the family of Achan is stoned for his folly (7:18, 24).

The daughters of Zelophehad, like Rahab, are responsible for preserving their ancestral household. On the basis of a promise by Moses they are given an entitlement among the brothers of their father (Josh. 17:3-4). The lot and the line of the father (*'ab*) are thereby preserved.

In the distribution of the land, Moses is said to have allotted the entitlements (*naḥelot*) on the other side of the Jordan (Josh. 13:32). The allocation at Gilgal, however, is portrayed as the work of Joshua, Eleazar the priest, and the heads of the ancestral households in the tribes of Israel (14:1). The heads of the ancestral households (*ra'še 'abot*) are depicted here as authority figures who, like Joshua, the model head of an ancestral household, play a role in determining allotments and boundaries.

Although the land allotments are said to be made to the various ancestral families (*mišpeḥot*) throughout the book of Joshua (e.g., Josh. 15:1), those who are designated as having the authority over the distribution of these allotments include the heads of the ancestral households (14:1; 19:51). There are no specified heads of the larger social groupings such as the ancestral family (*mišpeḥah*) or tribe (*maṭṭeh*). Special authority seems to lie with the heads of the ancestral households.

It is the heads of the ancestral households of Levi who come to Joshua, Eleazar, and the heads of the other ancestral households to negotiate cities for the Levites (Josh. 21:1). In the dispute over whether the tribes of the Transjordan were faithful to YHWH in building a huge altar beside the Jordan, ten chiefs accompany Phinehas, son of Eleazar, to meet with the tribes. Each head is specifically identified as "the head of an ancestral household among the clans of Israel" (22:14; author's translation).

The question of faithfulness to YHWH as the ruler who owns the land Canaan and who must be so recognized is placed here in the hands of a priest and the heads of the ancestral households. It is precisely to these heads (Josh. 22:21) that the tribes of the Transjordan make their confession of faith and faithfulness. They assert that the altar they have built is a testimony to their children that their families have a portion in YHWH, and presumably therefore also in YHWH's land (22:25, 27).[25] Phinehas and the heads of the family households accept the confession and report their findings to the rest of Israel (22:30-33).

Thus the heads of the family households are viewed as symbols of social power participating in the allocation of lands and acting as monitors of faithfulness to the God of the land. The ideology of Joshua establishes the ancestral households of Israel as the nucleus of the community and the heads of these groupings as the responsible leaders in the wake of Joshua's example.

In the two assemblies that conclude the book of Joshua, the heads (*ra'šim*) are included in the list of leaders present (Josh. 23:2; 24:1). This is probably an allusion back to the heads of the ancestral households involved in the land distribution (14:1; 19:51), although some suggest a connection with the heads of the groups established by Moses in the wilderness (Exod. 18:25).[26]

It is probably not accidental that allusions to the ancestors (*'abot*, Josh. 1:6; 18:3; 21:43; 24:2, 6, 17) provoke association with the ancestral households (*bet 'aboth*) and so promote their status. Joshua, after rehearsing the history of God's people from the time of the first fathers (*'abot*, 24:2), is presented as warning the people about the dangers of serving the gods of the ancestors (24:14) and so, making his own confession, Joshua declares that he and his ancestral household will serve YHWH exclusively (24:15).

Joshua is thereby depicted as encouraging other households and community leaders to put away the gods of the ancestors and follow his example. The response of the people is to acknowledge that YHWH is

---

25. Von Rad, *Old Testament Theology*, 299.
26. Koopmans, 277.

indeed the God who brought "us and our fathers" from Egypt to Canaan (Josh. 24:17 RSV). Clearly, the reference to ʾabot here (24:14) is not confined to the ancestors (as in 24:2), but includes all the ancestral households who came to Canaan. The ideology of Joshua, while promoting the status of households in social decision making, also presents them with the challenge to follow the model of Joshua and the households gathered at Shechem.

If ancestral households or families believe the task is beyond them, they have the assurance and example of Joshua. If they follow the law of Moses, renounce Canaanite deities, and avoid Canaanite wives, then they become invincible (Josh. 23:6-13). Israelite households need only remember the unequivocal word of Joshua, "For the LORD has driven out before you great and strong nations; and as for you, no one has been able to withstand you to this day. One of you puts to flight a thousand, since it is the LORD your God who fights for you, as he promised you" (Josh. 23:9-10).

RIGHTS AND RESISTANCE

The ideology of the book of Joshua supports the rights of each tribe, ancestral family, and ancestral household to its divinely approved lot in YHWH's land. The ancestral households, as the hope of Israel, are represented as having special responsibility and are given encouragement to pursue their rights to the land allotted them.

Joshua is given no more right to land than any other ancestral household. All his house gets is a small town, even though the decision of Joshua and his ancestral house to choose YHWH is the model for all Israel (Josh. 24:15).

The Levites play an important role in the book of Joshua (Josh. 3:3; 8:33), although they do not seem to have the same status as the guardians of the law that they hold in Deuteronomy. It is Joshua who reads the law (8:34) and inscribes the words of the law (24:25-26). The entitlement (naḥalah) of the Levites is the priesthood (18:7), the offerings of fire (13:14), and YHWH, their God (13:33).

Even though the Levites are said to have no land entitlement (Josh. 13:14; 14:3, 4), their ancestral families also receive lots consisting of cities and adjoining pasture lands (21:1, 3, 4, 8). The Levites take the initiative in gaining lots with limited land. Their entitlements, however, must be taken from the prior allocations of the other tribes on whose goodwill they are presumably dependent.

The Canaanites are accorded no rights to land in the opening conquest narratives. The rhetoric portraying the Canaanites as the big bad enemy to be annihilated is typical of ancient conquest accounts.[27] Beyond the ideal of total conquest, the book preserves the reality of Canaanite resistance. The Canaanites are survivors.

The modes of resistance demonstrated by the Canaanites include cunning, compromise and acknowledgment of the conquerors' deity, as in the case of Rahab (Josh. 2), maintaining control of strategic fortified cities (11:13; 15:63; 16:10; 17:12-13), and total commitment to the Israelite cause, as in the case of Caleb (14:6-15).

The book of Joshua's account of the Gibeonites' survival is a dramatic resistance story (Josh. 9). The Gibeonites use the techniques of cunning, deceit, and diplomacy typical of resistance narratives. They pretend to be aliens from a distant land and hide their true identity as the enemy within. They make a peace treaty with the Israelite leaders and confirm it in the breaking of moldy bread.[28]

When the ruse is discovered, the Israelite crowd wants blood. Joshua, as the model of just leadership, hears the case of the Gibeonites. Ironically, they quote the law of Moses that all inhabitants of the Promised Land should be destroyed and throw themselves on Joshua's mercy (Josh. 9:24-25). Joshua "saved them from the Israelites" (9:26) and consigns them to being slaves in the "house of my God" (9:23).

The Canaanites have no right to land; it has all been allotted to Israelite families. The Canaanites survive as forced laborers (Josh. 9:23; 16:10; 17:13; Deut. 20:11), a role viewed as appropriate to their cursed status and enforced by Solomon (1 Kings 9:20-21). These narratives, suggests Niels Lemche, reflect ideological messages for later generations of Israelites to justify their hostile treatment of unwanted non-Israelite elements in the land.[29]

27. Younger, *Ancient Conquest Accounts*, 65.
28. Younger, *Ancient Conquest Accounts*, 200–204, cites accounts of ruses in conquest narratives of the ancient Near East, but these do not negate the function of the Gibeon episode as a resistance story preserved in the ideology of Joshua.
29. Niels Peter Lemche, *The Canaanites and Their Land: The Tradition of the Canaanites* (Sheffield: JSOT Press, 1991), 120, 165.

The Canaanite survivors are not to be trusted. They are likely to use nonmilitary resistance strategies to subvert Israelite control of the land. A key strategy is intermarriage (Josh. 23:12). If Israelites marry Canaanites, YHWH will not continue to drive out the surviving nations. It is hard to drive out and destroy people with whom you have inter-married.

Thus the Canaanites are described as "a snare and a trap for you, a scourge on your sides, and thorns in your eyes," which will lead only to Israel losing the land (Josh. 23:13). Although the Canaanites show a remarkable capacity for survival and persist in parts of the land, no for-mal right to possess land is acknowledged. Allegiance to YHWH, the jealous God of Israel, means condemnation for Canaanite deities and households.

SUMMARY

The ideology of the book of Joshua upholds the symbol of the land as a cluster of family allotments to be possessed by those with the courage and initiative to do so. Figures like Rahab, Caleb, and the daughters of Zelophehad are held up as models of faithfulness and initiative. The supreme example is Joshua, the faithful servant of Moses, who con-quers the land for his people and subsequently upbraids them for not conquering and possessing their individual family allotments.

In the text of Joshua, the land of Canaan is specifically YHWH's land, which YHWH gives to the people of Israel as promised to their ancestors. YHWH is ruler of heaven and earth; YHWH is also presented as a warrior god, especially interested in helping the Israelites drive out and destroy the Canaanites in YHWH's land. Joshua is portrayed as the model soldier in the campaign against the enemy. Although the enemy are accorded no rights, many of them survive as symbols of resistance by virtue of their cunning, confession of faith, or strength.

The ideology of the book of Joshua also promotes the capacity of ancestral households and families to take the initiative, claim their allot-ted land, and rely on YHWH as the divine warrior to overcome all odds. It is the ancestral household, not the priesthood, the Levites, or prefig-ured royalty, that is being upheld as the hope for Israel. These house-holds are entitled to the royal lands of Canaan. In this utopian vision,

Joshua leads the way when he and his ancestral household "choose YHWH" (Josh. 24:15; author's translation).

The book of Joshua, then, seems to be a campaign document designed to encourage landless ancestral households and families, whether in exile or in Israel, to claim the royal lands once allocated to them but not now in their possession. The narrative of the book of Joshua provides an ideological charter for these ancestral households to choose YHWH and take matters into their own hands.

CHAPTER 5

Land as YHWH's
Personal *nahalah:*
A Prophetic Ideology

Land is one of the central themes in the ideologies of the classical prophetic books of Israel. In the book of Jeremiah, above all, the land is at the heart of a distinctive ideology portrayed as arising amid the ugly politics of the years surrounding the fall of Jerusalem. In an age when life without the land seemed unthinkable, the book of Jeremiah was depicted as promoting an ideology that was tantamount to treason.

It is my contention in this study that the ideology of the book of Jeremiah[1] promotes what might best be described as a symbiotic relationship among YHWH, the land, and the people of Israel. This ideology, espoused by a group demanding allegiance to YHWH alone, promotes a theology designed to negate a revival of Baalism; this doctrine justifies Jeremiah's pro-Babylonian politics and an ideal vision for restoration of the land in the distant future.[2]

An early version of this chapter appeared under the title "The Suffering Land: Ideology in Jeremiah," in *Lutheran Theological Journal* 26 (1992): 14–26.

1. My study works with the book of Jeremiah as a whole, recognizing that much of the text may reflect a Deuteronomic stage of transformation. The central ideology identified in this paper is based primarily on materials generally accepted as the work of the prophet Jeremiah. There is, I believe, a basic continuity between the ideology in the recognized oracles of Jeremiah and the final form of the book. Cf. W. Thiel, *Die deuteronomische Redaktion von Jeremia 1–25* (Neukirchen-Vluyn: Neukirchener Verlag, 1981); P. Diepold, *Israel's Land* (Stuttgart: Kohlhammer, 1972). In the last analysis, it is the book as a literary production that we must analyze and whose message is addressed to an implied audience.

2. Norman Gottwald, "Social Class and Ideology in Isaiah 40–55: An Eagletonian Reading," *Semeia* 59 (1992): 43–57, attempts an ideology of Isaiah 40–55 using the approach of Terry Eagleton, *Criticism and Ideology: A Study in Marxist Literary Theory* (London: Verso, 1976). My approach focuses on the land as a normative image promoted in the ideology of the text and does not seek to differentiate the several modes of production that typify many Marxist readings of the text.

YHWH's close personal bond with the land in the book of Jeremiah
is recognized by Walther Zimmerli, who contends that

> The frequent use of the designation "my heritage" (*naḥalah*) already
> marks it as characteristic of Jeremiah's speech. And it is the use of this
> designation to refer almost indistinguishably to the land and to the people
> that the close connection between this, God's land, and the people called
> by God is recognised. In the cultic defilement of God's land, Israel
> encroaches on God's own possession and compels him to pass judgement
> on people and land.[3]

My investigation of land ideology in the book of Jeremiah involves
an analysis of the central images related to the land as YHWH's
naḥalah, the social, cultic, and political dimensions of polluting the
land, the powerful motif of the prophet experiencing the suffering of the
land with YHWH, and the vision of the redeemed land with a new
social order.

YHWH'S OWN *NAḤALAH*

A central symbol of this intimate bond among YHWH, Israel, and the
land is *naḥalah,* usually translated rather inadequately as "inheritance."
A *naḥalah* is a specific allotment or entitlement, usually of land, that
has continuity with the past and ties with a sacred heritage.[4] In the tri-
angle of close relationships reflected in the book of Jeremiah, the land is
both Israel's *naḥalah* (Jer. 17:4) and YHWH's *naḥalah* (2:7). Israel, as
YHWH's people, however, is also YHWH's *naḥalah* (10:16), and
YHWH is Israel's "allotted portion" (*ḥeleq,* 10:16; author's translation).
YHWH, Israel, and Canaan are destined to belong together in a god-
land-people symbiosis.

The early chapters of the book of Jeremiah focus on Canaan as
YHWH's personal *naḥalah.* YHWH has inalienable tenure over the
land. Canaan is YHWH's own possession, a domain always destined to
be YHWH's land. As with the *naḥalah* of a peasant like Naboth
(1 Kings 21:3), the established bond between the owner and the land

---

3. Walther Zimmerli, "The 'Land' in the Pre-Exilic and Early Post-Exilic Prophets," in
Understanding the Word, edited by James Butler et al. (Sheffield: JSOT Press, 1985),
253–54.
4. On the basic concept of *naḥalah* as "entitlement" or "allotment," see the excursus following chapter 2.

overrides all other considerations. Family continuity, in the possession of its *nahalah,* is jealously guarded at all costs.

This *nahalah* concept in the text of Jeremiah seems to be informed by the tradition found in the Song of Miriam. The key verses read:

> You brought them in and planted them on the mountain of your own *nahalah,*
> the place, O YHWH, that you made your abode,
> the sanctuary, O YHWH, that your hands have established. (Exod. 15:17; author's translation)

Canaan was the *nahalah* for which the people of YHWH were destined after being delivered from the Egyptians. It was YHWH's own *nahalah,* YHWH's land and sanctuary.[5] This land was the vineyard chosen for "planting" Israel, YHWH's choice vine (Jer. 2:21; 31:27-28). The impression given is that prior to Israel's arrival the land was empty, free of all encumbrances, and ready for planting.

In the background lies the memory that Baal also claimed to have a domain as "my entitlement" (*nhlty*).[6] A jealous rivalry between YHWH and Baal over who was entitled to claim Canaan as their rightful *nahalah* is promoted through Jeremiah's vehement condemnation of Baal and Canaanite fertility rites (e.g., Jer. 2:8, 23 and often). YHWH won the right to claim Canaan as a *nahalah* by conquering the forces of chaos at the Sea of Reeds (Exod. 15:1-8).[7] And having taken possession of this *nahalah,* YHWH jealously guards it as a personal plot.

Also in the background is the ancient tradition that in the distant primordial past, Elyon apportioned a *nahalah* to each of the nations of the earth (Deut. 32:8-9; cf. Jer. 3:19; 12:14-17). This involved not only a division of peoples on earth according to the number of the divine beings (*bene 'el*) in heaven but also a fixing of the "boundaries" of these peoples. Each nation had its patron deity and its apportioned territory, its "allotted portion" (*heleq*). Lands were primordial allocations from on high. YHWH's allotted *nahalah* was Israel, both the land and the people (Deut. 32:9).

---

5. Cf. R. J. Clifford, *The Cosmic Mountain in Canaan and the Old Testament* (Cambridge: Harvard University Press, 1972), 139.
6. Arthur M. Brown, "The Concept of Inheritance in the Old Testament," Ph.D. diss., Columbia University, 1965, 183.
7. Habel, *Yahweh Versus Baal.*

The governing image in the opening oracles of the book of Jeremiah is of YHWH as a landowner, perhaps even a peasant landowner, bringing Israel to a pristine home to be YHWH's virgin bride (Jer. 2:2; cf. 31:4) or beloved child (3:19). Unlike other nations who may have possessed their allotted lands long ago, YHWH first acquires a people to locate in this land. More particularly, YHWH brings Israel from the distant land of Egypt to enjoy "my land" and "my *nahalah*" (2:7). On the way, YHWH's bride experiences harsh and alien desert lands (2:6).

By contrast with these wilderness lands, YHWH's land is rich and prosperous, full of good things to eat. God's land is like Eden, a land of plenty (*karmel*) and pleasure (Jer. 2:7; 12:10). In particular, the land is fertile, and YHWH jealously guards its fertility. YHWH is the owner who sends the rain, cherishes the land, and nurtures it as a vineyard (3:3; 5:24; 31:12). In this context the focus is on YHWH as source of fertility rather than creator of earth (cf. 14:22).

With painful nostalgia, YHWH remembers granting the Israelites a personal land for their home. In the original allocation of lands, there were apparently options (as in Deut. 32:7-9). YHWH, like a devoted father, chooses the very best *nahalah* on earth for this favorite child:

> I thought
>> how I would set you among
>>> my children,
>> and give you a pleasant land,
>>> the most beautiful *nahalah* of all the nations.
>> And I thought you would call me, My Father,
>>> and would not turn from following me. (Jer. 3:19)

YHWH had hoped to keep this *nahalah* in the family, that Israel would call YHWH father and not be a stranger in the father's land (14:8).

The intimate land-god-people relationship is also reflected in the anguished cry of Jeremiah 2:31. YHWH, who had brought Israel through the wilderness and lands of deep darkness (Jer. 2:6) to a beautiful *nahalah*, cries out in anguish,

> Have I been a wilderness to Israel,
> or a land of thick darkness? (2:31)

YHWH identifies with the land, as if YHWH was the luxurious land to which Israel was brought as a bride, only to be treated personally as a wasteland.

Another metaphor that reflects this symbiotic relationship between land, YHWH, and people is that of YHWH "planting" a people in the land (cf. Exod. 15:17). YHWH's *nahalah* is a garden or vineyard. Like a devoted peasant, YHWH carefully plants the people of Israel. YHWH's people are "a choice vine, from the purest stock" (Jer. 2:21; cf. 5:10; 8:13; 11:7). Israel is the vine and God's abode is the vineyard (cf. Isa. 5:1-4). Israel is "holy to the LORD, the first fruits of his harvest" (Jer. 2:3).

The imagery of these passages highlights YHWH's claim to the land as YHWH's own personal *nahalah* and abode, vineyard, and plot. YHWH is the owner, caretaker, and source of its fertility. Israel is brought to this rich home of YHWH, not to be a slave, a household servant (Jer. 2:14), or a poor peasant. Rather, Israel is given a highly privileged position. Israel is described as a bride, a favorite child, and a choice vine. From YHWH's point of view, Israel was accorded the highest status and given the best land, YHWH's own *nahalah*. Land, god, and people were united in a privileged intimacy.

The rhetoric of this idealized memory leads the audience to identify with YHWH as the deserted groom (Jer. 2:32) and forgotten father (3:19-20). Canaan is remembered as an idyllic land and Israel as a faithful partner. Here there are no allusions to the Canaanites, whose ways presumably polluted the land before Israel's advent. Nor is there any reference to the heavy hand of YHWH, the warrior groom, evicting these indigenous peoples. These traditions are suppressed in the interest of a governing ideal. If Canaan is indeed God's own *nahalah,* it was once pure, rich, fertile, and holy. In the sacred abode of YHWH, presumably only pure stock could be planted (2:2-3). In the ideology of the book of Jeremiah, the land as YHWH's abode is a pure plot and a personal *nahalah.* Canaan is virgin land for a virgin Israel!

At the same time, this ideology provides a genuine theological alternative to Baalism, which is depicted as popular in Jeremiah's day. YHWH was not just a distant deity ruling from the heavens or the divine hero of Israel's history. Rather, YHWH was bound up with the land, custodian (*ba⁽al*) of YHWH's own *nahalah* and the true God of fertility (Jer. 5:24). The text of Jeremiah underscored YHWH's intimacy with

the land without implying that the earth was a mother goddess or that
fertility required a divine consort. The book of Jeremiah's ideology
thereby undercut the claims of Baalism.

In spite of YHWH's intimate bond with the land of Canaan as a personal *nahalah*, YHWH's locus and power are not confined to that land.
YHWH claims to be the creator of heaven and earth (Jer. 10:12; 31:35),
a deity whose inescapable presence penetrates every secret corner of
heaven and earth (23:23-24). YHWH is also the deity who directs the
destiny of all nations on earth (1:10; 18:9; 25:15-29). The imagery that
frequently depicts the cosmic activities of YHWH, however, seems to
reflect the style of a storm deity who thunders from on high (25:30-31),
sends great storms (25:32), and stirs up the cosmic waters (10:13; cf.
51:15-16). Ultimately the land ideology of Jeremiah focuses on YHWH
as a jealous landowner who seeks to make YHWH's personal plot fertile and the people prosper as YHWH's own planting in that plot. This
nahalah is YHWH's preferred abode.

POLLUTING GOD'S LAND

The ideology of the book of Jeremiah also provided a basis for interpreting the downfall of God's people in terms of appropriate sin and
punishment. What offends and hurts YHWH, according to the text of
Jeremiah, is the polluting and defiling of this precious and pure
nahalah. Israel has dirtied YHWH's holy home. The initial indictment
of Israel in the opening trial (Jer. 2:4-13) makes this quite explicit:

But when you entered you defiled my land,
and made my *nahalah* an abomination. (2:7)

The ugly crime of which Israel here stands accused is not first and
foremost a breach of covenant (as in Jer. 11:1-8), but the pollution of
sacred land. It is not the violation of God's covenant law code that is
emphasized, but the defiling of God's precious personal property. This
pollution results from three contributing factors: religious, social, and
political.

The verb *defile* (*tama'*) generally has a cultic background appropriate
perhaps to the portrait of Jeremiah as someone from the priestly family
of Anatoth. In the first instance, this defilement is associated with a
return to Baal worship (Jer. 2:23) and a variety of fertility rites, which,

in the text of Jeremiah, YHWH finds disgusting. The language of the text almost becomes pornographic as the audience views a picture of Israel blatantly playing the prostitute "sprawled under every green tree" (2:20; author's translation).

The ironic tragedy for Israel is that, according to a tradition in the book of Leviticus, the land had already been defiled by the Canaanite peoples previously expelled from the land. In Leviticus this defilement is specifically linked to the religious, cultic, and social practices of these peoples (Lev. 18:25-30). In the ideology of the book of Jeremiah, the prior existence, activities, and character of the Canaanites are ignored. The precedent of a prior pollution is suppressed. Israel is guilty of profaning God's virgin land by taking the initiative in celebrating the cult of Baal.

The land pollution theme is developed through an extended adultery metaphor in Jeremiah 3:1-10. Israel is a faithless wife who has gone "whoring" after other lovers thereby polluting (ḥanap) the land (3:2). Judah, by pursuing the fertility rites of Baalism, has polluted the land "committing adultery with stone and tree" (3:9). This sexual rhetoric that the book of Jeremiah employs to evoke Israel's shame seems to be deliberately laced with crude and offensive sexual images.

YHWH, the faithful husband, had already divorced the faithless bride, Israel, for adultery. Now YHWH is threatening to divorce the fickle sister, Judah, who has only pretended to repent of apostasy (Jer. 3:6-10). Is there any hope after that? Judah has already polluted the land. Once Judah is divorced, there appears to be no chance of ever returning (3:1). After all, a divorced woman who returns to a man, according to Deuteronomic law, also pollutes the land (Deut. 24:1-4). "Would not that land be greatly polluted" (RSV) if God's people returned after Judah's adultery and divorce? (Jer. 3:1). Judah has had several husbands, including Baal. For this sullied wife to be again united with YHWH, her first and holy husband, it would mean profaning the land as never before.[8]

The ideological argument of this text of Jeremiah is clear. The blame for Judah's plight before, during, and after the Babylonian destruction of the land is placed on Judah's obsession with fertility cults. YHWH is

---

8. Walter Brueggemann, "Land: Fertility and Justice," in *Theology of the Land*, edited by B. Evans and G. Cusack (Collegeville, Minn.: Liturgical Press, 1987), 57.

the sole owner of the land and the source of fertility. Worshiping Baal and his consorts pollutes God's land. This polluting deed is the ground for expelling YHWH's own bride. A righteous God cannot tolerate a defiled abode forever.[9] YHWH would ultimately tolerate no rivals or compromise in this personal plot of land.

The rhetoric of the book of Jeremiah functions to convince the implied audience that Judah's pursuit of fertility rites was ludicrous and destructive. The text implies a party that promoted a popular ideology that preserved elements of the Canaanite religion as a meaningful vehicle for a full and fertile life in the land. According to this ideology, Baal was the source of prophecy (Jer. 2:8), a legacy of their ancestors (9:13), and the source of fertility. Apparently, allegiance to YHWH as the God of the exodus was not necessarily considered inconsistent with the affirmation of local practices associated with effective farming and husbandry in Canaan. This version of Baalism, it seems, claimed to offer a relevant ideology for God's people in a time of political turmoil.

The YHWH-alone party, as reflected in the text of Jeremiah, was unequivocal in its condemnation of this popular ideology. The ideology in Jeremiah that stressed the land-god-people symbiotic relationship could not tolerate any program that threatened the union. Baal, with his own land agenda, was therefore not portrayed as a minor aberration, but as a genuine threat. This version of Baalism could apparently claim hundreds of years of continuous blessing in the land. The Baal party had survived generations of persecution.

According to the book of Jeremiah, it was not the Canaanites who polluted the land, but Israelites embracing Canaanite fertility rites and establishing Baal as the ruler of the land. Baalism had defiled rather than fertilized the land. Such defilement of the holy *naḥalah* required radical action by YHWH as the true landowner (Jer. 9:11-16).

A secondary cause of land pollution seems to have been social injustice. Although the language of defilement reflects the cultic pollution associated with Judah's whoring after Baal, cultic and social corruption are closely linked. The harlot Judah, who lusts after lovers, also has "the lifeblood of the innocent poor" on her skirts (Jer. 2:34). The innocent poor are the oppressed in the land to whom YHWH pays special atten-

---

9. Robert Carroll, *Jeremiah: A Commentary* (Philadelphia: Westminster, 1986), 136.

tion. In the book of Jeremiah, Judah's treatment of the poor, the widow, the orphan, and the alien is the touchstone of justice.

In the famous temple sermon of Jeremiah 7, the prophet is presented as warning the people that this kind of injustice, coupled with the worship of other gods such as Baal, spells disaster. If the people amend their ways, YHWH promises to stay in the land and reside in the temple (Jer. 7:7). If they do not repent, YHWH is ready to destroy the temple of Jerusalem, as the house of God in Shiloh was once destroyed (7:14). Neither temple nor tradition would save Judah if the people persisted in these defiling abominations.

In the oracles ascribed to the prophet in Jeremiah 5:20-31, Jeremiah's promotion of YHWH as the true God of fertility is juxtaposed with a cry against exploitation of the poor by the wealthy. The lack of good rains (5:24-25) is the result of the sleek and fat who neither judge the case of the orphan justly nor "defend the rights of the poor" (5:28, author's translation; cf. 9:4-6). Survival and prosperity in the ideology of Jeremiah are dependent on denouncing Baal, acknowledging YHWH as the true source of fertility, and never gaining prosperity at the expense of the poor.[10]

Condemnation of social injustice in land matters, found in the book of Jeremiah, reflects the prophetic tradition evident in the books of other prophets of justice, such as Amos. The text of Amos presents the prophet's relentless condemnation of the upper classes as related to their exploitation of the land at the expense of the tenant farmers (Amos 8:4-6). In Amos 5:11, for example, the prophet condemns the rich landowner for demanding payment in wheat, which the tenant farmer could not afford, and appropriating the income to construct an elaborate house and plant pleasant vineyards.[11] As in Jeremiah, the text of Amos is represented as announcing that this injustice will mean exile "away from his land" (Amos 7:11), a land that will be "parceled out by lot" to aliens (Amos 7:17; author's translation).

The pollution of the land is also linked in the text with Judah's political alliances. Politics and idolatry were partners in the ancient Near East. By seeking political security through powers such as Egypt or

10. For the links between justice and fertility, see Brueggemann, "Land: Fertility and Justice."

11. Max Polley, *Amos and the Davidic Empire: A Socio-Historical Approach* (Oxford: Oxford University Press, 1989), 133ff.

Assyria, Judah was effectively forsaking YHWH as the pure fountain of
living water (Jer. 2:13-19). The ideology of the YHWH-alone group
implied in the text of Jeremiah included the belief that becoming
involved in seeking aid from foreign powers was tantamount to idolatry,
whether or not the recognition of specific deities was part of the deal.
To seek help from Egypt or Assyria was to challenge YHWH's capacity
to protect the land in the face of impending military might.

The result is a land laid waste, profaned by the path of foreign armies
across sacred soil (Jer. 2:15). Judah flits from one impotent lover to
another, from Egypt to Assyria, unaware that the consequence will be
shame and not security, disgrace and not prosperity (2:36-37; 30:14).
The folly of this political policy was exposed with the fall of Jerusalem.
The ideology of the YHWH-alone supporters was apparently vindicated. By seeking other alliances, Judah's alliance with YHWH was
vitiated and the land violated. Ejection of the faithless wife from
YHWH's defiled abode is viewed as a just punishment (11:15). Judah
deserved double damnation for polluting "my *naḥalah*" (16:18).

THE SUFFERING LAND

The polluted land is not merely some defiled object that can be dis-
carded. Rather, the land is a victim who suffers intensely as a result of
the crime and the punishment of Judah. The land is personified, not as a
goddess or mother earth, but as a kind of personal extension of YHWH,
the owner of the land.

Much has been written about the anguish of Jeremiah as depicted in
the confessions ascribed to Jeremiah (e.g., Jer. 11:18-20; 12:1-6; 15:10-
18; 20:7-18). Relatively little attention has been given, however, to the
land itself suffering as a personified victim of human evils and divine
anger.[12] This theme of the suffering land is signaled already in the first
of the confessions. Jeremiah is portrayed as suffering with the land as he
cries:

How long will the land mourn,
    and the grass of every field wither?
For the wickedness of those who live in it
    the animals and the birds are swept away,
    and because people said, "He is blind to our ways." (Jer. 12:4)

12. Diepold.

The mourning (*ʾabal*) of the land here reflects first of all the anguish the land suffers because of drought and the loss of animal life (as in Jer. 14:1-6). Just as painful is the flagrant wickedness of the inhabitants, who boldly claim the divine landowner does not see what they are doing to YHWH's *naḥalah* and YHWH will do nothing about it (3:3-4; 5:12; 7:9; 12:4).

This reference to the suffering land is the prelude to an extended oracle on the land as victim (Jer. 12:7-13). In the rhetoric of this oracle, both YHWH and the land suffer as the implied audience is moved to compassion for the landowner and the land.

The complex imagery of this oracle reflects the orientation of the opening chapters of the book of Jeremiah. Judah is God's beautiful bride; YHWH's *naḥalah* is designated "the beloved of my heart" (Jer. 12:7). The land is YHWH's allotted portion (*ḥeleq*, 12:10, cf. Deut. 32:9), a cherished vineyard in whom the vigneron once delighted (Jer. 12:10). Now the desolate vineyard "mourns to me" (12:11), the landowner, and no one seems to hear the cry (4:28). Landowner and land are joined in pain.

The land is a victim of rampaging shepherds who have no place in a vineyard (Jer. 12:10, 12). Whether these shepherds are Israelites (23:1-3) or alien rulers is secondary. God's lovely home has suffered abuse from those in power. Judah has become so rebellious that YHWH has been forced to abandon the people and the place loved so dearly (12:7-8). The jealous husband and landowner now "hates" this bride for defiling the husband's house (12:8).

The repeated use of the term *naḥalah* in this passage (Jer. 12:7, 8, 9) seems to be deliberately ambiguous and further underscores the symbiotic dimension of the land-god-people relationship.[13] *Naḥalah* seems to refer to both land and people, both the precious possession of YHWH and YHWH's chosen inhabitants. Now the wild beasts are called to devour what is left of YHWH's household (12:9). YHWH's *naḥalah* has become both victim and prey.[14]

In the extended oracle against the prophets, Jeremiah's agony is again linked with the suffering of the land (Jer. 23:9-12). The mourning of the land is presumably a reference to a drought. The disaster is the result of

13. E. W. Davies, 354.
14. Cf. Ronald Clements, *Jeremiah* (Atlanta: John Knox, 1988), 84.

a curse brought by YHWH, the source of fertility, on a land full of "adulterers." Once again it seems that the turning of God's people to other deities, presumably fertility gods, has provoked the curse. This does not make the pain any less cruel. YHWH's land suffers because it harbors adulterers instead of housing a faithful bride.

The suffering of the land at the hands of YHWH's bride is ultimately overshadowed by the land's suffering at the hands of Israel's enemies. The constant cry is that God's plentiful land has become an uninhabited "desolation" (Jer. 6:8), a silent wasteland (7:34), and a lifeless "wilderness" (9:10). YHWH's *nahalah* will be empty. YHWH speaks personally to the land, letting the land know of the disaster planned against the people (6:19). YHWH's cry of anguish against the evil king, Coniah, is addressed directly to YHWH's own plot in the triple exclamation, "O land, land, land!" (22:29).

The audience is summoned to wail and lament over a land devastated and deserted even by travelers, a land from which birds and animals have fled (Jer. 9:9-10). And the audience is invited to explain why the land is ruined and laid waste like a wilderness (9:11). The answer is again that Judah has forsaken YHWH and turned to Baal. Any association with Baals who claimed to be "owners" (*baᶜalim*) was an affront to YHWH who claimed to be the sole owner (*baᶜal,* 9:12-13; cf. 3:14; 31:32).

The prophetic judgment oracles of the book of Jeremiah could well have focused strictly on the deeds of Judah and the appropriate disaster. But the ideology of the book of Jeremiah is grounded in Canaan as YHWH's personal *nahalah.* The fate of the land is as important as the fate of the people. The suffering of God's land is as tragic as the suffering of God's prophet; neither deserves to be the victim of divine wrath. The rhetoric of this anguish is nowhere more heartrending than in the sequence of oracles about the enemy from the north in Jeremiah 4.

The opening oracle is a warning signal announcing that the foe from the north is on the march to make the land an empty "waste" (*šamma*), where cities have no inhabitants (Jer. 4:5-8). The response of God's people will be to wail and lament (4:8). The leaders will be appalled because they were so wrong. The text even has Jeremiah believing that God has deceived this people through such misguided leaders (4:9-10).

A series of images depicts the terrifying and relentless march of the

foe from the north to Jerusalem, the heart of YHWH's *nahalah* (Jer.
4:11-18). Stage by stage the prophet is depicted as viewing the
approaching doom until it reaches its target, to "your very heart" (4:18).
The prophet then explodes with anguish, almost as if he were YHWH
suffering the devastation of the land:

> My anguish, my anguish! I writhe in pain!
>   Oh, the walls of my heart!
> My heart is beating wildly;
>   I cannot keep silent;
> for I hear the sound of the trumpet,
>   the alarm of war.
> Disaster overtakes disaster,
>   the whole land is laid waste. (Jer. 4:19-20)

This portrait of the overwhelming pain of God's prophet is not
focused on the fate of the foolish people who have provoked this
disaster, but on the precious land of YHWH that suffers such ugly
devastation.

The full force of this traumatic suffering is felt in the famous vision
of Jeremiah 4:23-26. The audience senses the agony of the creator as the
creation returns to the chaos, darkness, and desolation of the primordial.[15] Creating a land and sky has been in vain. The land is becoming
waste and void as in the beginning. The sky is losing its light. Life is
disappearing. And the "plentiful land" (*karmel*) to which YHWH
brought the people of Israel (2:7) is becoming a desert (4:26). The cosmos is a victim of YHWH's anger, an anger provoked by the folly of
YHWH's people.

The interpretation of this cosmic vision that follows (in Jer. 4:27-28)
is sometimes dismissed as an anticlimax, a somewhat less inspired edi-
torial addition. These verses make it clear, however, that this vision is
linked with the future desolation of God's land (4:7). The devastation of
YHWH's *nahalah* will be of such proportions that land and sky will
perform the rites of mourning. The destructive word of YHWH will
reverse the creative word that once effected creation.

The ideology of the book of Jeremiah consistently focuses on the fate
of the land. The people have polluted YHWH's own "plentiful land"

---

15. Cf. Michael Fishbane, "Jeremiah 4:23-26 and Job 3:3-13: A Recovered Use of the
Creation Pattern," *VT* 21 (1971): 151–67.

(Jer. 2:7). God's anger is such that destroyers must be brought against the people who defiled this beautiful land. The people of the land must be expelled, and the land left empty and desolate (9:10-11). The land is a victim of Israel's pollution, Babylon's devastating armies, and YHWH's anger.

In the suffering of the land as a victim, of the people as exiles, and of YHWH as ruler of both, the depth of the tragedy is brought home. The suffering land ideology highlights the personal anguish of all three partners in the land-god-people relationship. In symbiosis, when one suffers, all suffer.

REDEEMING THE LAND

In the political realities surrounding the fall of Jerusalem and the exile of people from Judah to Babylon as outlined in the text of Jeremiah, the ideology of the prophet seemed to play into the hands of the enemy. According to this ideology, the land had to be purged and cleared of its defiling inhabitants. The Babylonian enemy was interpreted as the divinely appointed agent to perform this thankless task (Jer. 21:4-10; 25:8-14; 29:4-7). Jeremiah's famous scroll addressed to Jehoiakim summarizes this divine plan to destroy the land, to use Babylon as the agent of destruction, and to give the land a rest (*šabat*) from humans and beasts (36:29).[16]

When the city was under siege, the text has Jeremiah publicly announcing that YHWH had given the city into Babylonian hands and that the inhabitants would go into exile (Jer. 34:1-3). When the siege was over, Jeremiah was given a choice of home by Nebuzaradan, the Babylonian captain of the guard, who recognized Jeremiah's role in the Babylonian victory; Jeremiah could well have been viewed as a Babylonian agent or a traitor by his contemporaries (as in 38:4). Nebuzaradan makes a bold offer to Jeremiah that reminds us of God's words to Abraham (Gen. 12): "See, the whole earth is before you; go wherever you think it good" (Jer. 40:4; author's translation). The Babylonians thought they ruled the whole earth and could offer

---

16. In spite of the use of the verb *šabat* in Jeremiah 36:29, the text of Jeremiah does not seem to be alluding to the tradition of Chronicles and Leviticus 25, which links the exile with the need to give the land its sabbaths. For the text of Jeremiah, the exile is to be seventy years, not fifty years of sabbaths.

Jeremiah any abode, but he chose to stay behind in a desolated and polluted land. Why?

In a vision of the two baskets containing figs (Jer. 24), Jeremiah is presented as predicting that God's plan will be fulfilled by those in exile. They are therefore considered the good figs. God's plan is eventually to bring them back to this personal plot of land and "plant" them once again (24:6). The ideology of the book of Jeremiah thereby supports the future rights and status of those in exile. Those who are left in the polluted land will be sent all kinds of disaster until they are "utterly destroyed from the land" (24:10). Yet Jeremiah chooses to stay behind in a defiled and conquered land about to become a sheer desolation. Why?

In the letter to the exiles, Jeremiah is reported as urging those in Babylon to prepare for an extended stay and to develop an appropriate strategy for survival. This required that they be fruitful in marriage, plant gardens for subsistence, build solid houses, and seek the peace (*šalom*) of the city (LXX: "land") of their Babylonian masters (Jer. 29:5-7).[17] YHWH's plan was eventually, after seventy years, to bring the exiles home to Judah (29:10). In the ideology of Jeremiah, the exiles can cite the oracles of Jeremiah to justify their privileged status. Those in Judah have no future; they are figs too rotten to eat, too rebellious to redeem. Yet Jeremiah chooses to stay with the bad figs in a land with no immediate future. Why?

Given the ideology of the book of Jeremiah, the text's presentation of Jeremiah's politics as pro-Babylonian in orientation and the dire predictions of doom for all who remained in God's land after the fall of Jerusalem, why is Jeremiah presented as staying behind in Canaan? Why does Jeremiah join a party that seems to hope for survival in Judah when he had previously stressed Babylon as the locus of divine hope? The narrative of Jeremiah's land purchase (Jer. 32) seems to provide an answer consistent with the ideology of the book.[18]

The narrative commences with a new inquiry from King Zedekiah as

17. Cf. N. J. Rubinger, "Jeremiah's Epistle to the Exiles and the Field in Anathoth," *Judaism* 26 (1977): 85; Wang, M. Chen-Chang, "Jeremiah's Message of Hope in Prophetic Symbolic Action," *South-East Asia Journal of Theology* 14 (1972).
18. Whether this incident is historical or paradigmatic, as Carroll, *Jeremiah*, 622–23, proposes, the ideology of the future promoted in the account is significant.

to why Jeremiah keeps preaching such a treasonous message (Jer. 32:1-5). Why does Jeremiah preach that YHWH is giving Jerusalem into the hands of Babylon? This "why" sets the stage for the story and draws the audience into the discussion. Jerusalem is under siege, the rest of Judah is already conquered, and Jeremiah is supporting the Babylonians.

Jeremiah is approached by a relative called Hanamel to purchase a piece of land in Jeremiah's home village of Anathoth (Jer. 32:6-8).[19] Jeremiah then purchases the property and follows quite meticulously the legal and social practices required for such a purchase (32:9-15). Several key factors need to be taken into account if we are to appreciate the narrative portrait of this action:

1. Jeremiah's pro-Babylonian stance and his bold oracles announcing that YHWH was the one giving Jerusalem over to the Babylonians could be considered as so much rhetoric by the implied audience. An offer to purchase a plot of land in the hands of the enemy could put him to the test. Was he, in fact, a traitor ready to benefit from the plight of his own family? In spite of being hesitant about the initial message from YHWH, the text has Jeremiah interpreting Hanamel's coming as the word of God. To buy, it would seem, was to defy his fellows and to court the fate of a traitor.

2. The land being purchased was not represented as real estate on the open market. The land was specifically property to which Jeremiah had the right of redemption (Jer. 32:7). According to the land laws of Leviticus,[20] when a relative gets into difficulties, the next of kin is first given the opportunity to purchase the land to keep it in the family (Lev. 25:25-28). This land, it seems, is part of the ancestral family *naḥalah,* which has now been desecrated by foreign control. As such, this piece of land is a symbol of all the land of Canaan as YHWH's *naḥalah,* now polluted by Judah and devastated by Babylon. Closer relatives presumably do not want to risk buying land in enemy hands.

---

19. Whether this is a redemption proper (buying back property already sold to a third party) or pre-emption (buying property from a kinsman before it is put on the open market) does not change the symbolic significance of the deed. Jeremiah is depicted as redeeming the land. For the debate, see Raymond Westbrook, "Redemption of Land," *Israel Land Review* 6 (1971): 368–69; and *Property and the Family,* chapter 3; Dybdahl, 132–41, who argues that, in the light of Leviticus 25, Jeremiah leases the land.
20. See the discussion on Leviticus 25–27 in chapter 6.

It is the "traitor" Jeremiah who chooses to become a redeemer and keep the land in the family.

3. By purchasing this field (*sadeh*) in Anathoth, the prophet Jeremiah is represented as a paradigm of hope, like Abraham. Both obtain a "field" located in alien territory. Both "buy" the field according to a specified legal practice. Both obtain a piece of land that is the earnest of a promised land. Whereas in the Abraham narratives the future land is a friendly host country,[21] in the text of Jeremiah the future land is being destroyed by the enemy. Yet for Jeremiah, a fragment of the land is preserved as a reminder of YHWH's return to this *naḥalah*. Jeremiah is introduced as the first Israelite to own land in the anticipated new order for Israel.

4. Jeremiah's symbolic act is interpreted as a promise that "houses, fields and vineyards will again be purchased in this land" (Jer. 32:15; author's translation). This land, rather than Babylon, will proffer long-term hope for God's people. Interpretations are provided in the rest of this chapter of Jeremiah to clarify this hope. Once again, the text anticipates the fall of Jerusalem into the hands of the Babylonians. The Babylonians are now identified as the power employed by God to purge Jerusalem with fire, thereby removing all of the Baals and polluting abominations (32:26-35). In time, the privileged exiles will return to the land to dwell securely and serve YHWH with a true heart (32:36-41).

According to this narrative account, Jeremiah stays behind in Canaan because his ideology also embraces a stubborn vision that beyond the pollution, beyond the purging, and beyond the exile there will be redemption, a restoration of the land-god-people relationship of the idealized past. The land will be redeemed, God's people will return home, and YHWH will again plant the people in YHWH's own *naḥalah*.

The land, once pristine, pure, and prepared for YHWH's bride, must again be emptied, purified, and prepared for the return of YHWH's transformed people. The empty vineyard will again be planted with choice vines.[22]

---

21. See the discussion of Abraham's relation to the people of the land in chapter 7.

22. On the myth of the empty land in the book of Chronicles and elsewhere, see Robert Carroll, "The Myth of the Empty Land," *Semeia* 59 (1992): 79–93.

The image of once again sowing, building, and planting God's people in the land reiterates the symbiotic relationship between the people and the land. Both are YHWH's *nahalah,* both are to enjoy houses, fields, and vineyards. The seed to be sown is both the seed of humans and the seed of animals that will repopulate the land (Jer. 31:27; cf. Hos. 2:23). YHWH is depicted as the virile source of fertility impregnating the land with seed. YHWH will once more "plant" this people: "I will set my eyes upon them for good, and I will bring them back to this land. I will build them up, and not tear them down; I will plant them, and not pluck them up" (Jer. 24:6; cf. 31:28).

The people whom YHWH once planted in the land (Jer. 2:21; 11:17) will one day return home to their *nahalah* (3:18) and be planted anew (31:28). The same promise is even made to the so-called bad figs who could remain in Judah with impunity, but only if they accepted Babylonian rule as God's will and did not flee to Egypt (42:10-12). A pro-Babylonian politics is presented as essential to survival in the land, whether for those left behind or for the elite in exile.

A NEW ORDER IN THE LAND

Who will benefit from this return to YHWH's *nahalah* in the distant future? Where will the power lie? Who will control the land? It is interesting that the book of Jeremiah has the hero disappear into Egypt, leaving no progeny or organized YHWH-alone party behind him. His only disciple is Baruch, who has no more than the promise of survival (Jer. 45:5). Jeremiah is depicted as a figure with political self-interests for the future. Yet the survival of the book that bears Jeremiah's name is a production that testifies to the perpetuation of an ideology by a group that clearly has political aspirations.

The priests in the land are the repeated target of the prophet's fierce condemnation in the text of Jeremiah (Jer. 2:8; 5:31; 14:18). The defilement of the land is linked to the fact that the priests who are supposed to know the law and "know me" do not even ask "Where is YHWH?" (2:8; author's translation). Yet in their arrogance they claim that the "law shall not perish from the priest" (18:18 RSV). The priests and prophets are represented as joining forces to facilitate Jeremiah's execution (26:7-9). Neither the priests nor the prophets who ply their trade throughout the land are viewed as having any knowledge of YHWH or

YHWH's law (14:18). Understandably, therefore, these priests and prophets are not viewed as central to Jeremiah's ideology for the new social order in the land,[23] even though they were a significant force among the elite of the exilic community.

Instead, the power that comes with knowledge of YHWH, the power that comes with knowing the law, the power once claimed as the prerogative of the priests and prophets, will belong to all God's people, from the least to the greatest (cf. Jer. 9:2, 5). In the words of YHWH's proclamation of the new order, "I will put my law within them, and I will write it on their hearts; and I will be their God, and they shall be my people. No longer shall they teach one another, or say to each other, 'Know the LORD,' for they shall all know me, from the least of them to the greatest" (Jer. 31:33-34).

This egalitarian aspect, where the people know YHWH, seems to promote the image of a new community, all of whom are intimate companions of YHWH and invested with inner authority. This new community is designated the people of a new covenant (Jer. 31:31-34). Significantly, YHWH speaks of the relationship with Israel under the old covenant as that of Israel's *baʿal.* As *baʿal,* YHWH is both husband of this people and owner of the land. YHWH, not the local baals, is to be lord of this *naḥalah* and its tenants.

This new community is to be planted afresh in YHWH's *naḥalah* (Jer. 24:6; 31:27-28; 32:41). The new order will be possible in the redeemed land because all the people will have the knowledge of God in their hearts. The link between a changed heart, a new covenant, and a new planting in the land is made explicit in one of the sermons, which comments on the significance of Jeremiah's redemption of the family land (32:36-41; cf. 31:27-34). This required change of heart was signaled early in the book of Jeremiah. God's people must start anew by breaking up fallow ground and not sowing among thorns (4:3), and they must circumcise their hearts in faithful obedience to YHWH (4:4). The image of breaking new ground again reflects the close associations that are cultivated between people and land, according to the ideology of the book of Jeremiah.

---

23. Those verses (Jer. 33:14-26), which postulate a Levitical priesthood in the reorganized Israel, are clearly a later addition; they are not found in the LXX version of the text of Jeremiah.

Central to this ideology is a future when all people, from the least to the greatest, will know YHWH. This knowledge, however, does not necessarily require social equality. The least and the greatest, the prince and the pauper, will presumably still be represented in the land, but no longer "greedy for unjust gain" (Jer. 6:13). Those who return to possess the land are not only the elite in exile; the great company returning "to their own country" (31:17) will also include the blind and the lame, the young and the old (31:7-17). They will all have a right to enjoy the fertility of the new land. Just who will have a right to own land in the new order is not specified. Nor is there any consideration of what has happened to the family lands while the elite were in exile.

The principle enunciated earlier in the book of Jeremiah still stands: knowledge of YHWH, rather than wealth or riches associated with the royal elite, counts before God (Jer. 9:22-23). And that knowledge of YHWH is to be evident in the justice and righteousness in the land. Royalty as it had been known had to be terminated and a new order initiated.[24] If there were to be leaders in the future, they would feed their people on the very knowledge of YHWH that the people themselves possessed (3:15).

In the ideology of the book of Jeremiah, the concept of the just monarch that was so freely abused under the royal ideology of the Israelite monarchs is redeemed.[25] After condemning the monarchs of Judah for exploitation of the people, the poor, and the land (e.g., Jer. 21:11—23:4), YHWH promises to be the shepherd and raise up a new Davidic line to "execute justice and righteousness in the land" (23:5). The land will again experience that justice for the alien, the orphan, the poor, and the innocent, which guarantees peace, prosperity, and purity (cf. 22:3-5). The land will experience a reversal of those injustices that once defiled YHWH's personal plot.

Crucial to any future for Israel is the need to experience landlessness again, to die to the land. Before YHWH invests the people with new hearts and new knowledge, they must lose the most precious possession they ever had, YHWH's own plot of land. It is precisely those people

24. Walter Brueggemann, *Old Testament Theology: Approaches to Structure, Theme, and Text* (Minneapolis: Fortress, 1992), chapter 14, explores the significance of Jeremiah 9:22-23 (Hebrew) as a repudiation of the traditional royal ideology in Israel.
25. See the discussion on the royal ideology in chapter 2.

who are taken into exile and lose their land whom YHWH "regards as good figs" (Jer. 24:5; author's translation). YHWH's action is not based on their intrinsic goodness, their remarkable change of heart, or their potential as the "educated" of the community, but on YHWH's grace. YHWH chooses them, YHWH gives them a heart "to know" their God, and plants them again in YHWH's own *nahalah*. Without death from land loss, there is no new beginning in the land.

Ultimately the ideology of the book of Jeremiah does not offer a constitution for a totally new social order, but presents images hinting at the restoration of an idealized past order where everyone will know YHWH personally as they once did when Israel was first a bride (Jer. 2:2). In that society YHWH, as the source of fertility, will bring glorious prosperity to all the people (31:10-14). "Their life shall become like a watered garden" (31:12) and even the once derided priests will enjoy "their fill of fatness" (31:14). The vision is one of a new age when YHWH as the landowner will celebrate the fertility of YHWH's *nahalah* with one and all. The restored symbiotic bond among YHWH, people, and land will mean economic prosperity and social justice.

SUMMARY

An intimate bond exists between YHWH, Israel, and the land, a bond that might be characterized as symbiotic. YHWH is bound to both land and people. The land seems to be personified as a third party in this relationship. The land is YHWH's chosen *nahalah* from among all lands; the people are "planted" in YHWH's personal plot of land. No other deity or power is tolerated in this union.

The charter for this claim is the story of YHWH bringing a people as a virgin bride through the wilderness to a pure land, free from Canaanite pollution. YHWH, who is also creator of earth and heaven, is to be acknowledged as the sole source of fertility in the land prepared for this people.

According to this ideology, when God's people violate their relationship with YHWH through cultic or social evils, they pollute the sacred land. The land becomes a tragic victim, suffering at the hands of God's people and God's anger. The once beautiful *nahalah* of YHWH mourns and laments like a howling wasteland. The land suffers desolation and the people suffer exile; YHWH suffers with both land and people. In this ideology, YHWH seems as vulnerable as the land. Yet suffering land loss is necessary if Israel is to have a future with YHWH; the land must also be purified and completely emptied again. Even Jeremiah is removed from the land.

The agent of this purging action is Babylon. In the short term, therefore, a pro-Babylonian politics is demanded. The long-term vision looks beyond Babylon, life in exile, and the empty land to a new beginning created by YHWH alone. In that day the ideology of the implied YHWH-alone party will be vindicated.

Any new beginning with YHWH will include YHWH's personal *nahalah.* This beginning will involve a "new planting" in the land and a "new heart" in the people of the land to re-establish the intimacy and purity of the original land-god-people relationship. Any new order will involve all YHWH's people, from the least to the greatest, knowing YHWH in a personal way that was once reserved for priests and prophets. And the greatest, under YHWH the shepherd, will know how to execute justice in the land and for the land.

This new beginning is planned for the "emptied" land of Canaan. Those privileged to possess this land—and perhaps participate in emptying it—are the elite Israelites in exile.

CHAPTER 6

Land as Sabbath Bound:
An Agrarian Ideology

In a recent study on the biblical jubilee Jeffrey Fager contends,

> When the priests edited the jubilee legislation, they were looking toward
> the establishment of a new economic order, the old order having been
> swept away by the Babylonians. Had they chosen to do so, they could
> have included the cities in the jubilee's provisions. However, since the
> purpose of the jubilee seems to have been to preserve the economic
> integrity of the peasant farmer, there was no need to protect urban prop-
> erty from alienation.[1]

Whether or not the jubilee legislation of Leviticus 25 reflects a time
when a particular economic order was swept away by the Babylonians
is highly debatable. What is widely recognized, however, is that the
jubilee legislation is promoting a radical social order designed to preserve the economic integrity of the landed peasant farmer.[2]

To appreciate this agrarian land ideology, in this chapter we use the
literary unit of Leviticus 25–27 as the basis for our analysis. Apart from
the obvious thematic connections between these chapters, there are
structural indications that these chapters represent a literary and legisla-
tive unit.[3]

---

1. Jeffrey Fager, *Land Tenure and the Biblical Jubilee* (Sheffield: JSOT Press, 1993), 88-
89.
2. We use the term *peasant* or *peasant farmer* in this study to refer to the head of an
Israelite household who owns and works traditional lands. Cf. Fager, *Land Tenure*, 84.
This common usage is to be distinguished from Bernhard Lang's ("The Social
Organisation of Peasant Poverty in Biblical Israel," *JSOT* 24 [1983], 85) designation of
the peasant as one who maintains a household but who works the land for the landowner.
3. Leviticus 25–26 seems to be a literary unit framed in 25:1 and 26:46 by the only two
references to Sinai up to this point in Leviticus. See Christopher J. H. Wright, *God's*

Our analysis of this ideology involves an examination of the dominant images associated with land, YHWH's particular relationship to the land, the land sabbath, the law of jubilee, and the relative rights to land of the various groups in the envisaged social order presented in the text.

LANDOWNER AND LAND TENURE

In Leviticus 25–27, YHWH is the one who owns the land. No one can alienate any portion of YHWH's land by selling it, exchanging it, or transferring permanent tenure to others. YHWH controls the use of the land, ownership of the land, tenancy on the land, conditions of land usage, and the seven-year cycle of production. In short, YHWH is the owner and the custodian of the land.[4]

If so, the Israelites are ideologically represented as tenants rather than owners of the land they cultivate. This is made explicit by their designation as *gerim* and *tošabim* on YHWH's land (Lev. 25:23). These terms are appropriately rendered in the New Revised Standard Version as "aliens" and "tenants."[5] The Israelite tenants owe allegiance to YHWH as their landowner, patron, and benefactor. As tenants, they apparently have no right to permanent tenure or ownership of the land itself. They hold their traditional lands in trust by virtue of the generosity of their divine patron.

The land (*'ereṣ*), which these tenants hold for their landowner, is specifically agricultural land: fields to be sown, vineyards to be tended,

People in God's Land (Grand Rapids: Wm. B. Eerdmanns Publishing Co., 1990), 149–50. Leviticus 27 appears to be an explicit continuation of those matters that "belong to YHWH" and are under the control of the priests including persons, animals, property, and tithes. This chapter is also framed by a reference to Sinai as the venue and symbol of the land laws (27:34).

4. Relevant dissertations on land tenure include Stephen Herbert Bess, "Systems of Land Tenure in Ancient Israel," Ph.D. diss., University of Michigan, 1963; Brown; Dybdahl; Jesudason Jeyaraj, "Land Ownership in the Pentateuch," Ph.D. diss., University of Sheffield, 1989.

5. The term *gerim,* often rendered "sojourners," is more appropriately translated "resident sojourners" or "immigrants" in most contexts. See Frank Spina, "Israelites as *gerim,* 'Sojourners,' in Social and Historical Context," in *The Word of the Lord Shall Go Forth,* edited by Carol Meyers and M. O'Connor (Winona Lake, Ind.: Eisenbrauns, 1983), 321–35. The noun *tošabim,* which is based on the verb *yšb,* "to reside," is frequently coupled with *sekirim,* "hired laborers" (e.g., Exod. 12:45; Lev. 25:6, 40). The *tošabim* then seem to refer to resident workers or tenants. Cf. Bess, 112, who indicates that Damaschke, as early as 1922, rendered the term "feudal tenants."

and produce to be harvested.[6] This land, whose usage may be bought, sold, or redeemed under the landowner's conditions of tenancy, is the agricultural land that provides life and sustenance for those who tend it. The Israelite tenants, it seems, are peasant farmers, and YHWH is custodian of arable lands.

Which model of land control enables us to interpret the role of YHWH as the custodian of the land and helps us clarify the ideology of the text? In what sense is YHWH the landowner? Is YHWH viewed as a rich urban landowner, a tribal head, or a monarch? Or is the model that of the sanctuary abode from which the deity controls the land?

The image of YHWH as a wealthy urban landowner is unlikely in this context. YHWH seems to identify very closely with the peasant tenants in a way that suggests an alienation from the urban world. Those who dwell in walled cities may accumulate houses as property (Lev. 25:29-30), but they do not play a key role in the proposed land economy. The sympathy of the audience is not with the urbanites; it would be odd for them to view their landowner as a wealthy urbanite controlling the use of peasant land.[7]

The model of YHWH as a tribal head seems a more plausible option. According to this model, each tribe, ancestral family cluster (*mišpeḥah*), and ancestral house (*bet 'ab*) would receive and preserve land as its traditional entitlement (*naḥalah*) from YHWH.[8] Two references to the ancestral family may support this option (Lev. 25:10, 41). Significantly, however, the key term for tenured land in this legislation in not entitlement (*naḥalah*) but acquired property (*'aḥuzzah*), a term more appropriate to nontribal tenure situations. Joseph, for example, assigns his brothers tenure over property (*'aḥuzzah*) in the land of Egypt (Gen. 47:11). In the year of jubilee each peasant returns "to his property" (Lev. 25:13) rather than to his entitlement (*naḥalah*), as in the tribal context of the book of Judges (Judg. 21:23-24; cf. Josh. 24:28).

It is possible that the concept of property held by each family includes, in the background, the tradition of specific land allotments to

---

6. Cf. Jesudason Jeyaraj, "Ownership, tenancy and care of land in Leviticus 25–27," typescript. Gillis Gerleman, "Nutzrecht und Wohnrecht: zur Bedeutung von 'Achuzah und Nachalah,'" *ZAW* 89 (1977): 316–17, argues that the term *'aḥuzzah,* which is used for landholdings in Leviticus 25–27, refers specifically to cultivated land.

7. Cf. Lang.

8. See chapter 4 and the excursus on *naḥalah* following chapter 2.

particular ancestral families and tribes as outlined in Joshua 13–20. It is striking, however, that this law in Leviticus, which proclaims that land-holdings are to be returned to their original owners in the year of jubilee, is nowhere linked with the tradition of these lands as entitlements to ancestral families when they entered Canaan.

A number of scholars have emphasized that YHWH does not function here as a typical ancient Near Eastern monarch.[9] YHWH does not distribute largesse to favorites, appoint administrators to monitor and control lands, or make the people rulers over the land on YHWH's behalf (as in Gen. 1:26-28). The only allusions to "ruling" are negative (Lev. 25:46; 26:17). There is no interest in gaining or maintaining a national territory under royal control. Nor does YHWH entrust the land to a monarch as the earthly appointee of an ambitious heavenly ruler. In sum, monarchy does not seem to be linked to YHWH as owner or to the mode of tenure chosen for the land.

The most likely model of land tenure associated with YHWH in this text is the widespread ancient Near Eastern custom of deities owning the land where their abode was located.[10] A specific area of land around the temple was under the direct control of the priests or temple functionaries. This temple estate could be large or small depending on the largesse of the ruler or the power of the priests. Beyond the temple estate itself, the entire land of a given nation or region could be claimed by the deity. The central sanctuary was often viewed as a sacred portion of the land representative of the whole land; the land, in turn, was viewed as extended sanctuary. To pay homage was to acknowledge the deity's ownership of the worshiper's land.[11]

Although the full force of this model of land tenure will become apparent in the deliberations that follow, the summary demand to "keep my sabbaths and reverence my sanctuary" (Lev. 26:2) brings together

---

9. Bess, 87ff.; Brown, 83ff.; Wright, 62; Robert North, *Sociology of the Biblical Jubilee* (Rome: Pontifical Biblical Institute, 1954), 62ff.

10. Bess, 3–4.

11. Wright, 60; Ronald Clements, "Land and Temple: A Significant Aspect of Israel's Worship," *Transactions of the Glasgow Oriental Society* 19 (1961–62): 16–28; idem, *God and Temple* (Oxford: Blackwell, 1965), 52–54; Bess, 3ff. Cf. Joel P. Weinberg, "Die Agrärverhältnisse in der Burger-Temple-Gemeinde der Achamenidenzeit," *Acta Antiqua* 22 (1974): 473–86, who distinguishes between three land-related groups in the temple community: temple staff who worked temple-owned land, peasants who worked temple-owned land, and peasant tenants who worked land not owned by the temple.

the economic and the cultic connections with the land in a pointed way.[12] In this context, the sabbaths clearly include the land sabbaths and the years of jubilee that the tenants must observe (25:2-12).

What is the sanctuary (*miqdaš*)? The usual assumption is that the sanctuary is limited to a specific abode of the divine landowner in the midst of the tenants. The land tenure connection, however, suggests that another tradition, which designates the land of Canaan as God's sanctuary, may also be reflected here.[13] In Exodus 15:17, for example, the land of Canaan is designated YHWH's entitlement (*naḥalah*) and sanctuary (*miqdaš*), even before any shrine or temple is built in the land.[14] No images are to be erected anywhere in the land, presumably because the land is YHWH's sanctuary (Lev. 26:1). Although there may be links with other land tenure models previously outlined, the sanctuary model seems to be the dominant one, according to which YHWH owns and controls the land from within an extended sanctuary.

THE LAND SABBATH

The opening section of Leviticus 25 proposes legislation about a land sabbath for the Israelites (Lev. 25:1-7). That this legislation is intended to promote land reform is evident from the way it reinterprets quite radically the laws that preceded it.[15] This reform envisaged a new agricultural economy based on the premise that Israel's God is, in fact, a generous landowner who will bless the new economy if Israel adheres to the regulations announced for the new land program.

The opening clause specifies the contractual relationship between YHWH as landowner and the people of Israel as tenants.[16] The regulations of this contract apply "when you come into the land which I give

---

12. Cf. Gerhard von Rad, "The Promised Land and Yahweh's Land in the Hexateuch," in *The Problem of the Hexateuch and Other Essays*, ed. Gerhard Von Rad (New York: McGraw-Hill, 1966), 79-93. In Leviticus 19:29-30, the same juxtaposition of land, sabbaths, and sanctuary suggests that in this passage, too, the land may be viewed as an extended sanctuary and the sabbaths include more than the weekly sabbath.

13. Brown, 184-86; cf. Martin Noth, *Exodus* (Philadelphia: Westminster, 1962), 125-26. Note also Ps. 114:2.

14. Baal's domain is designated a "sanctuary" before Baal builds a temple; Norman Habel, *Yahweh Versus Baal*, 61-62. The temple is a symbol or replica of the land or sanctuary of the deity.

15. Cf. Jeyaraj, "Ownership, tenancy and care of land."

16. Cf. Orlinsky, 31-33, argues that *ntn* frequently has the technical and legal sense of "grant or assign tenure."

you" (Lev. 25:2 RSV). Here there is no theological reflection on an ancient promise to give the land of Canaan to the ancestors. The arable land is given explicitly to the recipients of the legislation, the people of God in the sanctuary of God.

The first and perhaps most important condition that the Israelite tenants must observe is keeping the land sabbath. More precisely, it is the land itself that must keep the sabbath. The agricultural land over which Israel holds tenancy is to keep its sabbaths "to the LORD." It is as if YHWH is addressing this law to the land itself, a land that is capable of responding to the way the Israelites handle it. The life of YHWH's own land is at stake.[17]

On the sabbath year, the land returns to its owner, to the LORD; the tenants have no rights or responsibilities in that year. By returning the land to its divine owner, the Israelites acknowledge their absolute dependency on the goodness and authority of their landowner. When the people, including the Israelites, were tenants of the pharaoh, they were expected to give one-fifth to their royal landowner (Gen. 47:24). In Leviticus 25, the divine landowner makes an even more radical demand, requiring that all cultivation be suspended every seven years. In that year the land—and presumably the owner—enjoys complete rest without the turmoil of tenants at work. It is as if YHWH and, indeed, the people of YHWH identify with the land in that year.

The land sabbath regulation, which requires tenants to desist from any form of cultivation or horticulture during the seventh year, interprets the ancient law of fallow in the covenant code of Exodus 20–23. This law reads: "For six years you shall sow your land and gather in its yield; but the seventh year you shall let it rest and lie fallow, so that the poor of your people may eat; and what they leave the wild animals may eat. You shall do the same with your vineyard, and with your olive orchard" (Exod. 23:10-11).

The law of fallow may have been based on sound agricultural experience and practiced elsewhere in the ancient Near East, but its promotion in the covenant code was linked with humanitarian ethics. The produce of the fallow fields was for the landless in society who had no other

---

17. The ecological nuance of Leviticus 25:2 is lost in a translation such as that of the Good News Bible, which reads, "You shall honor the Lord by not cultivating every seventh year."

means of income. Agriculture was to reflect principles of social justice, expressed as charity for the marginalized poor. Landed peasants, it seems, could rotate their fields so that one was left fallow every seven years. The practice was good for the productivity of the land and the welfare of village life.[18]

The land sabbath of Leviticus 25 reforms the ancient fallow law in several significant ways. The land, not the tenants, seems to be the primary subject of the sabbath requirement. The rationale given for this sabbath is not to provide charity for the landless poor or the marginal in society.[19] Rather, in the seventh year, the land reverts to its owner, to the divine landowner. The motivation given is religious. In the sabbath year, the fallow land is for the landowner rather than for the poor. Moreover, the land sabbath, unlike the fallow law, applies to all arable land during the sabbath year; every seven years all agriculture is to cease in the land.

Understandably peasants as well as urbanites would find the proposed regulation difficult to accept. How could an agricultural economy be sustained if all the land lies fallow once every seven years? What kind of security and forward planning are possible under such a system? Or as the audience in the text asks, "What shall we eat in the seventh year, if we may not sow or gather in our crop?" (Lev. 25:20).

The answer given is threefold: The Israelites will have economic security if they keep the pertinent ordinances of their landowner (Lev. 25:18), this economic security is to be found in the exceptional fertility of the land (25:19), and an extraordinary crop will be reaped every sixth year to compensate (25:21).

The link between Israel's obedience and a future on the land is a common theme elsewhere in the traditions of Israel (e.g., Deut. 6:10-15; 11:13-17). Here in Leviticus, however, the focus is on the land itself playing a role, yielding or not yielding its produce, depending on the relationship of the Israelites to their landowner (cf. Lev. 26:18-20). The land responds to the lifestyle of its tenants, to its sabbath years of rest, and to the blessing of its landowner. The land is a living reality with

---

18. Cf. Wright, 62; North, 144. Anthony Phillips, *Ancient Israel's Criminal Law* (Oxford: Blackwell, 1970), 75, quite rightly points out that if the fallow land was for the sustenance of the poor there would need to be land left fallow every year.

19. The humanitarian concern in the Holiness Code is associated with leaving the edges of the field and the gleanings of the harvest for the alien and poor (Lev. 23:22).

rights to be respected. In this section of Leviticus, it is not defilement of
the land by impure social mores that forces the land to spew out its
inhabitants (18:24-30; Num. 35:34), but a refusal to maintain the principles of agricultural economy being espoused by this legislation. The
evil here is exploitation of the land, not its defilement.[20]

Even more radical in this economic plan is a demand for allegiance to
YHWH, the landowner, based on YHWH's unique powers of fertiliza-
tion. During the sixth year of this agrarian program, the landowner will
"command" a blessing: the edict is addressed to the land. The result will
be an extraordinary harvest that provides enough food for more than
two years, or more specifically for the seventh, eighth, and the beginning of the ninth years of the economic cycle (Lev. 25:20-22).

Such a plan requires the whole society to be absolutely dependent on
the generosity and goodwill of the landowner, trusting in the capacity of
YHWH to produce an extraordinary crop in the sixth year as proof of
YHWH's miraculous powers. Baal could only be expected to fertilize
the land annually to provide a reasonable harvest. Placing faith in
YHWH's farm plan, however, would result in a new agricultural society
with a mandatory sabbath year, during which peasant farmers would not
be farming but presumably involved in other ventures about which we
can only speculate.

THE LAW OF JUBILEE

The law of jubilee, which follows the land sabbath law, introduces a
unique social institution designed to incorporate further regulations that
will govern this new economy and epitomize its ideology. This institution is known as "the year of jubilee," the fiftieth year following seven
cycles each of seven years (Lev. 25:8-9). A supernumerary sabbatical is
to be held after seven sabbatical years and publicly pronounced by the
blowing of a ram's horn, quite appropriately, on the day of atonement.

This jubilee involved a universal proclamation of *deror,* a kind of
economic amnesty in which all debts were forgiven, property was
restored to its owners, indentured slaves were released, and land repos-

20. On the defilement of the land motif, see Walter Brueggemann, "Land: Fertility and
Justice," 41–68; W. D. Davies, *The Territorial Dimension of Judaism* (Berkeley:
University of California Press, 1982), 18–21; Carroll, "The Myth of the Empty Land."

sessed by its traditional occupants.[21] The jubilee was thus a period of balancing this new agricultural society through acts of liberation, release, and restoration (Lev. 25:8-55).

The governing principle of the plan is that "you shall return, everyone of you, to your property" (ʾaḥuzzah, Lev. 25:13). This Hebrew term specifies legally acquired property. In ancient Israel, land could be acquired by purchase (Gen. 23:11-18), by assignment at the hands of a landowner or monarch (Gen. 47:11), or by tribal decree (Num. 27:4). The term ʾaḥuzzah normally designates acquired property used for cultivation. This term is to be distinguished from naḥalah, which is a wider concept covering any land or portion of land to which a person or group is entitled by charter, decree, allotment, or inheritance.[22] In the jubilee policy, each person is to return, it seems, to the acquired property over which he or she holds tenure under YHWH as landowner. The designation of peasant land as legally acquired property (ʾaḥuzzah) suggests the reality of individual ownership; this designation is quite striking in view of the ideology of the text, which characterizes peasants in ideological terms as "aliens" and "tenants" on the land of YHWH, the landowner (Lev. 25:23).

The text provides no indication of how this property was originally acquired from YHWH. The tradition of allocating land by lot to ancestral families and tribes, described in Joshua 13–21, is not cited as a charter for restoration of lands in the year of jubilee. The term naḥalah, usually associated with this tradition and with land entitlement, is avoided in this legislation.

The ideological implications of this policy are quite far-reaching. First, the policy provided a mechanism for deterring in the short term and preventing in the long term land monopolies or latifundialization, the process of land accumulation in the hands of a few landowners to the detriment of peasant farmers. This practice is roundly condemned by Isaiah: "Woe to those who accumulate house to house, and add field

21. See North; Sharon Ringe, *Jesus, Liberation and the Biblical Jubilee* (Philadelphia: Fortress, 1985). Moshe Weinfeld, "Sabbatical Year and Jubilee in the Pentateuchal Laws and Their Ancient Near Eastern Background," in *The Law in the Bible and Its Environment,* edited by Timo Veijola (Göttingen: Vandenhoeck & Ruprecht, 1990), 39–62, identifies a number of ancient Akkadian parallels to this kind of proclamation of liberty.
22. See the excursus on *naḥalah* following chapter 2.

to field, until there is no small landholding, and you have become pos-
sessors of land all by yourselves in the midst of the land" (Isa. 5:8;
translated by D. N. Premnath).[23]

Second, the peasant farmers, in spite of bad years, misfortune, debts,
or even bad management, were guaranteed a long-term resolution of
their situation. They or their family would eventually return to the
ancestral property, in the year of jubilee. The ideal of the peasant farm
economy would be thereby assured, and the trend toward control of the
land by the urban elite would be curbed (cf. Micah 2:1-2).

Third, interim resolutions of the peasant's situation were also possible. A kinsman, presumably someone from the same ancestral family,
could take over the land for a price until the peasant could repay or until
the year of jubilee (Lev. 25:25). Alternatively, if no kinsman could
redeem the land, individual peasants could themselves redeem the land,
should their fortune change (25:26-27). The process of redemption,
therefore, was an alternative to waiting until the year of jubilee and
achieved the same end.[24]

Fourth, any purchase of land did not mean permanent ownership or,
in contemporary terms, gaining title to the land. Instead, the proposed
practice involved buying the use or produce of the land until the next
jubilee year. The price was calculated on the possible number of crops
from that date until the year of jubilee, taking into account that no crops
were possible in sabbath years. Buyers were really obtaining a leasehold
or mortgage on the land for a predetermined period of years.[25]

Fifth, the planned agricultural economy would necessarily be cyclical,
based on the security of the traditional community rather than on ever-
increasing productivity or power. The forty-ninth and fiftieth years
would function something like a planned recession when no land, property, or personnel would be sold or exchanged in the agricultural sector.
All commerce related to property outside the cities would come to a halt.
In the fiftieth year all peasant families would start de novo on their own
properties, with the opportunity to make good, irrespective of the past.

23. D. N. Premnath, "Latifundialization and Isaiah 5:8-10," *JSOT* 40 (1988): 49–60. The
translation is that of Premnath, 49.
24. Fager, *Land Tenure and the Biblical Jubilee,* 94.
25. Cf. Bess, 120; Jeyaraj, "Land Ownership."

The jubilee economy was based on the ideological assumption that YHWH was the landowner. Not only was property to be returned to its assigned owners but also the arable land as a whole was to be returned to its divine owner. No land could ever be sold in perpetuity because the land was owned ultimately by YHWH. Each landholder was viewed as a tenant on God's own land.

Yet each tenant had a legal right to a particular parcel of arable land. This type of land tenure is therefore to be distinguished from patterns of communal ownership or the so-called "Asiatic mode of production,"[26] according to which tenants had no tenancy rights but were merely a community of slaves owned by the ruler of the land.

The full force of the jubilee ideology is reflected in the divine assertion that the Israelites are *gerim* and *tošabim* on God's land. These terms are often translated *strangers* and *sojourners,* expressions that are somewhat misleading. As designations of social groups, these Hebrew terms clearly imply those who lack the rights and permanency of the established members of the community. A number of scholars have shown that the *gerim* as a social group are equivalent to resident aliens or immigrants who emerge from a situation of social conflict.[27] The term *tošab,* which is commonly coupled with *sekarim,* "hired servant," is more appropriately rendered "sharefarmer" or "tenant," as in the New Revised Standard Version.[28]

In Leviticus 25–27, Israelite peasants, whatever their historical origins, are designated something like "immigrant tenants" who hold their land by the authority and goodness of YHWH, the landowner. Before God they have no inalienable right to the land; their future on the land is contingent on absolute allegiance to the requirements of the landowner. The land and the peasant are both inexorably bound by the sabbath principle governing the proposed land program.

There is no clear evidence that the jubilee program was ever implemented on a regular basis according to the agenda outlined in Leviticus

---

26. Fager, *Land Tenure and the Biblical Jubilee,* 91–93; D. Jobling, "Deconstruction and the Political Analysis of Biblical Texts: A Jamesonian Reading of Psalm 72," *Semeia* 59 (1992): 114.

27. See note 5 this chapter. Cf. Christiana van Houten, *The Alien in Israelite Law* (Sheffield: Sheffield Academic Press, 1991).

28. Cf. Bess, 112.

25.[29] This lack of historical evidence, however, does not negate the significance of the jubilee as an ideological symbol of a radical land reform
program promoting the rights of the peasant. The significance of that
symbol persisted in works like the *Book of Jubilees* and perhaps the
New Testament (Luke 4:19).[30] The restoration of lands and manumis-
sion of slaves by Nehemiah, although bound to a historically specific
situation, reflects the same spirit of concern for Jewish peasants who
suffered at the hands of nobles and officials (Neh. 5).

SECURITY AND LOSS OF TENURE

Following the regulations promoting an ideal agrarian society (Lev.
25), the text outlines conditions that would mean security or loss of land
tenure in God's land (Lev. 26). The condition specified in the opening
verses stands almost like a catch cry for the chapter: "You shall keep my
sabbaths and reverence my sanctuary: I am the LORD" (26:2). The
Israelite community is to keep the sabbaths, including the land sabbaths
and the year of jubilee, and to give due reverence to the extended sanctuary of their landowner.

If the Israelites are faithful to the requirements of their landowner,
they can expect a long list of agricultural, economic, and social blessings, including seasonal rains, fertile fields and trees, abundant harvests,
security and peace on the land, absence of wild animals and strife, victory over invaders, and increased progeny. Coupled with these blessings, the people can be assured that God will maintain the covenant with
them as a people (Lev. 26:11-13).

Two features of this portrait of blessings are especially relevant to
promotion of the peasant economy. The first is that YHWH, the
landowner, will have a dwelling or presence (*miškan*) in the midst of the

29. Robert Gnuse, "Jubilee Legislation in Leviticus: Israel's Vision of Social Reform,"
Biblical Theology Bulletin 15 (1985): 46, cites three reasons for arguing that the jubilee
was never practiced: There is no extant reference to its being practiced, tension with the
Deuteronomic Code, and the economic impracticality of the jubilee law. Cf. Fager, *Land
Tenure and the Biblical Jubilee,* 34–36. Weinfeld, "Sabbatical Year and Jubilee," 58,
however, does not rule out the possibility that in ancient Mesopotamia there was a cyclical amnesty as well as the one commonly announced upon the accession of a monarch to
the throne.
30. Margaret Rodgers, "Luke 4:16-30: A Call for a Jubilee Year?" *Reformed Theological
Review* 40 (1981): 72–82, is typical of those who question that Luke 4:16-30 has any link
with the jubilee year concept.

tenants (Lev. 26:11). YHWH will not, however, be confined to a fixed abode but will walk (*hithalak*) among the tenants, presumably as a demonstration of concern for the people of Israel. This walking of God in the land recalls the "walking" of God in the garden of the first peasant farmers (Gen. 3:8). Like Eden, the land is God's sanctuary. Here YHWH is no absentee landowner who resides in heaven and visits from above, or locates the divine name at a particular shrine; YHWH dwells in the land, walks through it, and celebrates its sabbaths.

It is also possible that *miškan* here refers specifically to the tabernacle, as elsewhere in Leviticus, and that the text envisages a rural future in which YHWH moves about the land in a tabernacle. This interpretation is supported by the fact that the same verb (*hithalak*) is used of the tabernacle moving about among the people of Israel before the temple was built (2 Sam. 7:6-7).

The second significant feature of these blessings recalls the action of God in bringing the Israelites out of slavery in Egypt. The goal of this exodus act is not only to bring the people to the land of Canaan (Lev. 25:38) but also to enable them to "walk erect" (26:13) as free, independent people in their landowner's sanctuary.

If, however, this peasant society does not give due recognition to its landowner and obey the sabbath regulations, the Israelites will suffer a succession of serious economic setbacks, culminating in exile. The exile of Israel, in this context, is closely linked to the belief that the people had violated the land sabbath laws and raped the land itself. If Israel will not give the land its rest, then God will impose an enforced sabbatical. The land belongs to YHWH and must be preserved. As noted previously,[31] the concept here is not identical with the belief found earlier in the holiness code that the land will vomit out its inhabitants if they defile the land by practicing certain sexual abuses (Lev. 18:24-30), even if the resultant expulsion from the land is the same. The focus here is on honoring the principles of the proposed land economy; to dishonor them is to exploit and abuse the land itself.

The disaster of exile can be reversed and the land redeemed if the Israelite people genuinely repent of their defiant ways and treacherous lives (Lev. 26:40-41). Their God will then remember the covenant made

31. See note 20 in this chapter.

with the ancestors, which is presumably the promise of a land. But more significantly God will "remember the land" (26:42). YHWH, the landowner, has a close bond with the land; it is YHWH's sanctuary. YHWH remembers people like Noah in his lonely ark. And YHWH remembers the land.

This gracious act of goodwill on the part of the landowner does not mean instantaneous return. The land is still bound by the sabbath principle and has priority. The land must first enjoy the numerous sabbaths of rest that it was denied under the tenancy of Israel. After the appropriate number of years, Israel may return to establish the social order envisaged in these laws. As a jealous landowner, YHWH desires responsible tenants who will maintain an attitude of reverence and concern for the very soil and soul of the land.

THE SOCIAL ORDER IN THE LAND

The land ideology of Leviticus 25–27 is linked with a specific social order that includes landed peasants who possess their land as a property (*ʾaḥuzzah*) held in tenure under divine ownership. These peasants may sell the use of their land in a crisis and redeem the land in due course. They possess a long-term right of return to their land.

Ancestral peasant households may include male and female servants or slaves, hired laborers, and tenants (Lev. 25:6). These households, which correspond to the traditional "father's house" (*bet ʾab*), represent a significant agricultural social unit, capable of cropping extensive ancestral property perhaps in the style of Boaz (Ruth 2). Leviticus 25:10 suggests, however, that the extended ancestral family or clan (*mišpeḥah*) is the secure social unit with which Israelite peasants were associated in the jubilee.[32]

Resident tenants (*tošabim*) and aliens or immigrants (*gerim*) have the capacity to prosper to the extent that when landed peasants suffer misfortune, they may sell their services to members of this social group

---

32. On *mišpeḥah*, see Norman Gottwald, *The Tribes of Yahweh*, 301–5, who describes this social grouping as "a protective association of extended families." Cf. W. Johnstone, "Old Testament Technical Expressions in Property Holding: Contributions from Ugarit," *Ugaritica* 6 (1969): 313. David Hopkins, *The Highlands of Canaan* (Sheffield: Almond, 1985), 256–61, sees the *mišpeḥah* as a cluster of families formed to spread risk and optimize labor in highland agriculture.

(Lev. 25:47-54). This group is also bound by the regulations pertaining to redemption and the year of jubilee.

Urbanites in walled cities could buy and sell houses according to regulations that were not subject to the law of jubilee. Urbanites, whatever their trade or profession, could accumulate wealth in the form of houses or through trade, but they could not become long-term landholders (Lev. 25:29-30). Towns without walls belonged to the village peasant community and were not subject to this special dispensation for urban property (25:31).

The Levites are only mentioned here in Leviticus. Their social role is not specified, but they are allocated cities as their possession. Houses they sell are subject to the law of jubilee and must be returned to their Levite owners. The open land around a Levite city is, however, inalienable and cannot be sold (Lev. 25:32-34).

Priests presumably tend the shrines (Lev. 26:31) in YHWH's extended sanctuary and may also hold land as property.[33] Land tenure for priests is not by traditional inheritance or allocation, as with the peasants, but by a process of consecrating traditional lands to YHWH (27:14-25). This was perceived of as an act of peacetime *ḥerem*, that is, dedication to YHWH by means of an allocation to the priests rather than by pursuing the scorched earth practice typical in YHWH's wars (cf. Josh. 6).

Who benefits from the social order of this land economy? The first and most obvious answer is the peasant farmers, who could retain long-term usage of the land within their extended families and be assured of economic stability in spite of fluctuating circumstances. Servants, hired laborers, land tenants, or resident aliens remain dependent on the welfare of the peasant household for their livelihood. Urbanites are left to their commercial ventures within their city walls.

Excluded from this portrait of a stable peasant society are urban landowners, monarchs, or their representatives. Where then lies the political power? The answer, it seems, is with the priests. The priests apparently monitor the economic laws of the proposed farm economy. The priests manage the sabbaths and jubilees that govern the new econ-

---

33. The fact that here priests hold property is remarkable because elsewhere in the Old Testament this does not normally seem to be the case. Elsewhere YHWH, not land, is the inheritance of the priests (e.g., Deut. 18:1-2).

omy. Because the jubilee is linked with the day of atonement and the sounding of the sacred horn (*šophar*), the priests are presumably responsible for proclamation of the jubilee year. The priests, moreover, can progressively acquire more and more lands on a permanent basis as traditional properties are dedicated to YHWH over the years. Thus, in the proposed land economy of Leviticus 25–27, the priests possess social, religious, and economic power in a land that is viewed as YHWH's extended sanctuary.[34]

Although there is a strong concern in this proposed social order to preserve the traditional landholdings of the peasants and maintain their independence over against rich landowners, the society is not truly egalitarian in the contemporary sense of the term. Laborers, servants, immigrants, and urbanites are excluded from gaining the same level of social standing as landholding peasants or priests. Powerful monarchs, chiefs, and urban landowners may have been removed from the top of the social order, but the rural workers at the bottom of the order remain dependent on the landed peasant farmers. Thus the common assumption that the Israelite peasant economy was truly egalitarian, while the Canaanite orientation was hierarchical, is too simplistic.[35]

The system of law in the jubilee complex, according to Yairah Amit, attempts to diminish the economic and social gaps between the members of society. He argues that this law reflects a struggle against "the phenomenon of economic inequality and against that domination and exploitation of one part of society by another."[36] This concern for social justice, however, is primarily focused on the peasant landholders who suffer misfortune and does not embrace household servants or slaves, for whom landownership was never a possibility.[37]

34. Fager, *Land Tenure and the Biblical Jubilee,* 98, goes so far as to claim that the priests were promoting this ideology, which especially maintained their status, but which they hoped to impose on the whole people and so revitalize the nation after the crisis of the exile.
35. On the peasant economy of the ancient Near East, see Lang.
36. Yairah Amit, "The Jubilee Law: An Attempt at Instituting Social Justice," in *Justice and Righteousness,* edited by Henning Graf Reventlow and Yair Hoffman (Sheffield: JSOT Press, 1992), 51.
37. Weinfeld, "Sabbatical Year and Jubilee," 42, points out that slavery was an assumed social situation in the Pentateuchal laws. Israelite landholders could sell themselves into slavery on account of personal debts. Such "slaves" are to be differentiated from household slaves, both foreigners and Israelites, who never possessed land but were a permanent part of the household.

The ideal of the peasant society depicted in Leviticus 25–27 is that peasant farmers will be completely free from domination by the urban elite. The cities would continue to function with their own set of property laws, but the peasants, under the jurisdiction of the priests, would have long-term security on the land. The urbanites would be segregated into their cities and have no control over peasant lands.

There is no clear textual evidence to assume that "the juxtaposition of villages and walled cities presupposes a balance between the Canaanite and Israelite way of life," as Fager contends.[38] Rather, the text seems to be the product of a later era in which the community reflected in the text is promoting a return to the ideals of an agrarian age. And those ideals embrace the nostalgic image of peasant land, rather than a chosen city, as the locus of YHWH's presence. YHWH's land and abode is the garden of Canaan.

It is not our task here to debate the precise historical situation that may have given rise to this ideology. Fager contends that the jubilee land laws were formed during the late exilic period by priestly writers.[39] It is plausible that the "poorest people of the land" (2 Kings 24:14; 25:12), left behind after the city leaders were taken into exile in Babylon, had a vision of land reform that guaranteed the future of peasant landholders freed from the domination of the monarchy and urban landholders.

It is just as plausible to argue that the text reflects an ideal of ancestral families in exile who hope to return to the land they once lost. Clearly the text of the sabbath law promulgates what Carroll calls "the myth of the empty" land.[40] The exile is interpreted as an act of YHWH rendering the land "desolate" to punish Israel for not keeping the sabbaths YHWH required for the land (Lev. 26:34-35). This feature would tend to support the argument that this ideology is being promoted by a community who has experienced exile.

SUMMARY

YHWH is the custodian and owner of all the land upon which rural Israelites are tenants; as tenants they hold their designated property in

---

38. Jeffrey Fager, "Land Tenure and the Biblical Jubilee: A Moral World View," Ph.D. diss., Vanderbilt University, 1987, 94f.
39. Fager, *Land Tenure and the Biblical Jubilee,* 38–39; cf. Amit, 57–58.
40. Carroll, "The Myth of the Empty Land."

trust. YHWH is not an absent ruler in heaven, but a local landowner who walks through the land and establishes a presence there; the land is YHWH's extended sanctuary. The ideal economy is a landed peasant economy governed by the sabbath principle; every seven years and every jubilee year the tenants return the land to their landowner for rest. Failure to uphold this sabbath-based land economy will result in the landowner ejecting the tenants so that the land will enjoy enforced sabbath years.

The projected land economy keeps the land usage in the hands of traditional peasant families and prevents large landholdings or land control by urban rulers or landowners. The proposed ideology does not promote a general principle of sharing the land, but specifies particular individuals as heads of traditional families, having the right to particular sections of God's land.

The controlling power in this land economy lies with the priests, who are responsible for upholding the sabbath principle; ultimately the priests are the only social group that can progressively accumulate land. The social model implied in this land economy means political power for priests, security for peasants, and dependency for slaves, hired laborers, and immigrant aliens; in short, the reform proposes an agrarian theocracy.

CHAPTER 7

Land as Host Country:
An Immigrant Ideology

Each of the ideologies discussed in the preceding chapters refers to the doctrine of land promised to the ancestors as a justification for Israel's claim to invade, conquer, dispossess, and settle the land of Canaan. The doctrine of promised land is fundamental whether or not, in a particular ideology, the ancestors were understood as the patriarchs, the exodus generation, or both. This doctrine is variously interpreted and enhanced to promote the vision of a given ideology. In this chapter we turn to the Abraham charter narratives, which provide an unexpected elaboration of this doctrine.

Does the ideology of these charter narratives correspond to the principles of one or more of the preceding ideologies, or do these narratives promote an ideology that has a different orientation? It is my contention that the Abraham narratives reflect a distinctive immigrant ideology that views the land as a host country and its inhabitants as potentially friendly peoples. The vision of the ideology in these charter narratives, I would argue, is in conflict with most of the ideologies, even though they also appeal to this promise doctrine as their charter.

I shall function with the Abraham narratives as a literary whole (Gen. 11:31—23:30), recognizing that whatever sources or traditions may have been part of the growth process,[1] we now have a text that presents

---

This chapter is a development of a 1992 article that appeared under the title "Peoples at Peace: The Land Ideology of the Abraham Narratives," in *Religion and Multiculturalism in Australia,* edited by Norman Habel (Adelaide: AASR, 1992), 336–49.

1. J. Van Seters, *Prologue to History: The Yahwist as Historian in Genesis* (Louisville: Westminster/John Knox, 1992), chapter 12, provides an overview of some of the major theories about how the promise traditions developed. The commonly used term "patriarchal narratives" embraces stories of both patriarchs and matriarchs in these traditions.

us with the Abraham story as a structured narrative in its own right and a cycle of episodes with a dominant viewpoint. I acknowledge the research of scholars such as Meir Sternberg, who have shown that in biblical narrative the ideological, historiographical, and aesthetic functions are closely intertwined.[2]

I am not interested here in reconstructing the social process that gave rise to the creation of the Abraham traditions, a process that George Mendenhall, for example, discerns in the "disintegration of the old tribal federation and the rise of the temporary empire."[3] John Van Seters's proposition, that the Yahwist is a historian who transposes the promise of land given to the exodus generation of Israelites back in history to the patriarchal period, is yet another theory of how traditions were combined in the development of the Abraham cycle of narratives.[4]

Nor am I concerned with hypothesizing about the specific historical audiences for which parts of the Abraham cycle may have been written, although many of the ideological thrusts seem to be relevant to the Israelites in exile in Babylon or later.[5] Rather, I identify and analyze the dominant land ideology of the text as addressed to the implied audience of the text as a whole.

I delineate the major elements of this ideology by analyzing the migration account, which introduces the Abraham cycle of narratives and depicts Abraham as an immigrant; the promise texts, which constitute the specific charter for this land ideology; the specific land covenant made with Abraham; the pattern of relationships between Abraham and the host peoples of Canaan; and the image of the God of the land revealed to Abraham.

THE MIGRATION NARRATIVE

An appreciation of the immigrant ideology of the Abraham narratives can perhaps best begin with an analysis of the migration account of

---

2. M. Sternberg, *The Poetics of Biblical Narrative* (Bloomington: Indiana University Press, 1985), 35–50.
3. George Mendenhall, "The Nature and Purpose of the Abraham Narratives," in *Ancient Israelite Religion,* edited by Patrick Miller et al. (Philadelphia: Fortress, 1987), 340.
4. Van Seters, *Prologue to History,* 239.
5. Van Seters argues, with some cogency, for an exilic date for the Yahwist. See also J. Van Seters, *Abraham in History and Tradition* (New Haven: Yale University Press, 1975), 264.

Genesis 11:31—12:9. Most studies of the Abraham saga commence
with the call of Genesis 12:1-3 as evidence of a remarkable act of faith
that leads Abraham to travel to some mysterious unknown land, led
only by the inner guidance of his God. When we consider the Abraham
story as a whole, however, the situation is somewhat different.[6]
Abraham's call to go to Canaan is actually part of a migration narrative
(Gen. 11:31—12:9), which can be broken into six elements:

- The plan of the Terah group to migrate from Ur to the land of
  Canaan
- The settlement of the Terah group in Haran
- The call to complete the migration to Canaan
- The journey of the Abraham household to Canaan
- The travels of the Abraham household through the host country of
  Canaan
- The establishment of sacred sites in the host country

As this narrative outline reveals, the plan of the ancestral household
of Terah to migrate to Canaan is a given; Canaan is not an unknown
destination, even if it may be an unknown quantity. There is no explicit
indication of why the Terah group leaves Ur and no evidence for the
expulsion, as Walter Brueggemann supposes.[7] The land of Canaan is a
land of opportunity and the goal of the migration plan. Abraham does
not flee from a land of evil but is part of a migration from one urban
center to another en route to a new land. Abraham and his household are
immigrants.

The settlement of the Terah household in Haran is passed over
quickly in the text. Abraham's stay is interrupted with an unexpected
summons from his God to separate from his father's family in Haran
and fulfill his father's original plan to migrate to Canaan, "the land that
I will show you" (Gen. 12:1). The catalyst for completing the migration
is identified in this text as YHWH, the God who thereby legitimates the
original plan of Abraham's father.

The migration narrative may offer a signal to an implied audience of
exiles in Babylon that they are not in a totally alien place. Their ances-

---

6. It is probably because this text has been regularly split, by assigning sections to the
Yahwist and the Priestly sources, that the migration pattern of the text as a whole has not
been fully appreciated.

7. Walter Brueggemann, *The Land*, 16.

tors came from that very land and have a kinship with its people. Ur, after all, was part of Babylon. Whatever the historical context that produced the migration narrative, the text reflects no sense of alienation between Ur and Canaan, as is often suggested. Ur is the old home country and Canaan the new host country; they are linked by the person and people of Abraham.

In Haran the Terah household is said to have "settled," which clearly suggests making that territory a new homeland. Terah did not merely "sojourn" in Haran. And the subsequent command of YHWH is for Abraham to leave the land of his ancestral household and go to a new land, presumably to settle there. Abraham migrates from one land to another; he is not depicted as one of the landless poor[8] or like one of the Israelites wandering uprooted and aimless in the wilderness, but as an ancestral hero led by God in search of a new land,[9] a hero who provides an ancestral bond between an ancient homeland and a new land. Abraham is portrayed as an immigrant, not a refugee.

Abraham's journey to Canaan with all his family and possessions happens without incident; the description of the journey concludes with the succinct but emphatic, "They set forth to go to the land of Canaan, and they came to the land of Canaan" (Gen. 12:5; author's translation). Canaan is clearly the land of destination and destiny. Significantly, the land seems open to migrants; there is no mention of any barriers set up by the inhabitants. Abraham migrates, it would seem, to a friendly and inviting land. Abraham is not yet in control of the land, but then neither is he threatened with domination or eviction by the rulers in the land. Canaan is depicted as a peaceful place to live, a welcome host country for immigrants and settlers. Abraham moves without constraint through the length and breadth of the land.

According to the migration narrative, Abraham passes "through" the land, an act that can hardly be dismissed as innocent sightseeing. It is precisely at this point in the text (Gen. 12:6) that the Canaanites, the indigenous inhabitants of the land, are introduced. The land is not empty, but neither is it hostile. Abraham freely surveys a friendly territory, belonging to the host people of the land, where he or his descen-

8. Bastiaan Wielenga, *It's a Long Road to Freedom: Perspectives on Biblical Theology* (Madurai: Tamil Nadu Theological Seminary, 1988), 137.
9. P. Miscall, *The Workings of Old Testament Narrative* (Chico, Calif.: Scholars Press, 1983), 17.

dants will stake a claim. These journeys through the land (12:6-9) are tantamount to mapping the territory associated with a future land claim. After separating from Lot, Abraham actually "walks through the length and the breadth of the land" at God's command to chart the promised territory (13:17) and thereby symbolically claims ownership. Yet no one seems to object; here the Canaanites are not depicted as enemies, as they are in most other biblical land ideologies.

At two places in the migration narrative, and subsequently at several others (e.g., Gen. 13:18; 21:33; 22:9), Abraham establishes sacred sites. These sites bind Abraham's seed to the land, because at these sacred locations the God of the ancestors is to be found. The ancient trails of the ancestors and the sacred sites they establish turn the territory into a storied landscape in which the history of Israel's beginnings is tangibly recorded. In this charted land the ancestors find their God, a God whose stories in the land precede the Abraham migration, and who performs the function of a welcoming host and a sustaining deity.

The characterization of Abraham as an immigrant is evident also from the use of the term *ger* and associated verbal forms. The term has been variously rendered "stranger," "resident alien," and the more archaic "sojourner." Frank Spina has argued, quite convincingly, that the term *immigrant,* which reflects the social factors and conditions associated with both the emigration and immigration process, is a more appropriate rendering.[10]

Abraham specifically identifies himself to the Hittites as a *ger* residing in their midst (Gen. 23:4). He is not an unwelcome alien or a passing traveler. He is the equivalent of an immigrant who chooses to put down roots and buy land on the terms of the host country. Abraham is also said to reside as an immigrant in Gerar (20:1) and in the land of the Philistines (21:34). It is by virtue of Abraham's status as an immigrant that Abimelech expects Abraham to deal justly with him and his land (21:23). The land of Canaan is specifically designated the immigrant land for Abraham and his seed (17:8).

THE PROMISE CHARTER

At two points within this migration narrative, programmatic promises from Abraham's God are introduced (Gen. 12:2-3, 7) that provide vital

10. Spina, 321-35.

clues for understanding the ideological viewpoint of the account. As a package, these promises provide the charter for a land ideology that is explicated in the following Genesis narratives.[11] In brief, these promises are that

- Abraham will become "a great nation."
- Abraham's "name" will become "great."
- Abraham will mediate "blessing."
- Abraham's seed will obtain "the land."

The promise that Abraham would become a great nation implies a future history in which the Abraham family will be transformed from a small social group into a political power with a controlling interest over the land. The land of Canaan will become the homeland of this great nation. The land is the launching place for national ambition; the promise is entitlement for national expansion.

The promise to make Abraham's name great is usually contrasted with the ambition of the people of Babel, who through unified political action sought to "make a name" for themselves and build a tower into heaven (Gen. 11:4). Their efforts ended in abject failure. A great name is not to be achieved through aggressive efforts to invade the abode of God on high. Instead, a great name is bestowed on the forefather of Israel at the discretion of the host deity of the new land below.

The preceding promises may reflect, in part, the language of royal ideology. David is said to have a great name (2 Sam. 7:9; 1 Kings 1:47). The monarch is potentially ruler of a great nation and the mediator of blessing to other nations (Ps. 72:17). The blessing power appropriated by monarchs is assigned in the Abraham narrative to the head of a household, the progenitor of a people. The locus of power has been shifted from the court to the community, from the monarch to the head of the household. The family of Abraham and his seed are to mediate blessing to other families: "Through you all the families of the earth will be blessed" (Gen. 12:3; author's translation). Abraham is given the land so that he can become a vehicle to bring blessing to other ancestral families.[12]

11. Claus Westermann, *The Promise to the Fathers* (Philadelphia: Fortress, 1980), provides a detailed explication of these promises.
12. On mediating the blessing, see especially Hans Walther Wolff, "The Kerygma of the

Giovanni Garbini suggests that God gives Abraham "the blessing of which in the ideology of the ancient Near East the king was the guarantor."[13] Van Seters extends this suggestion by arguing that "the Yahwist has democratised the royal ideology by applying it to the forefather of the people."[14] My analysis indicates that the locus of power and responsibility, which in other ideologies may rest with the monarch or the priest, here rests with the head of the ancestral household, of whom Abraham is the great paradigm. The land granted to Abraham is the location for exercising that power for blessing to others.

A comment needs to be made about the terminology of this promise. Abraham, who has just left his own "ancestral household" (*bet ʾab*) to become the ancestor of a new household, is to become the mediator of blessing to the "ancestral families" (*mišpeḥot*) of the earth.[15] The head of the smaller social group is to bring blessing to the larger social groups of the earth (cf. Gen. 18:18). In the immediate context, this means that Abraham is to mediate blessing to the ancestral families of the host country, including the Canaanites. In the wider context, the seed of Abraham has the potential to bring blessing to all nations of the earth. In the textual context, the promise that Abraham would establish his ancestral household remains fragile while he lacks a legitimate heir.

In a subsequent promise of YHWH, the audience is informed that Abraham will become the progenitor of "a great and mighty nation" (Gen. 18:17-19). His responsibility as the progenitor of this great people is to make sure that his household (*bet*) keeps the way of YHWH by doing justice in the land. The promise charter is linked specifically to Abraham as progenitor, who has left his own ancestral house (*bet ʾab*, 12:1; 20:13) to become the founder of a new ancestral house.

This promise that Abraham would become a "great and mighty nation" is not coupled with an ideology of dominating other nations, but with the ideal that "through him all the nations of the land (*ʾereṣ*) will be blessed" (Gen. 18:18; author's translation). Abraham's nation is to

Yahwist," in *The Vitality of the Old Testament Traditions,* edited by Walter Brueggemann and Hans Walther Wolff (Atlanta: John Knox, 1975), 41–46.
13. Giovanni Garbini, *History and Ideology in Ancient Israel* (New York: Crossroad, 1988), 79.
14. Van Seters, *Prologue to History,* 256.
15. On *bet ʾab,* see chapter 4, note 6; on *mišpeḥah,* see Norman Gottwald, *The Tribes of Yahweh,* 315–17, and chapter 6, note 32.

mediate blessing to all other nations of the *ʾereṣ*, a term that suggests both the land of Canaan and the whole inhabited earth. How this is to be achieved is not specified in the promise. Blessing, however, clearly implies imparting the power of life, a power often associated with monarchs and priests. This power includes fertility (17:16), economic growth (24:35), political control (24:60), and social importance (12:2; 17:16, 20). The nation of Abraham's seed is supposed to empower, not disempower, other nations of the host country.

Admittedly, anyone who curses Abraham, and presumably his seed, will experience God's curse. But the primary focus of the promises, as well as their explication in the narrative context, is on the role of Abraham and, to some extent, Jacob, mediating blessing without conflict. Abraham is to bring blessing to the land and not curse, peace and not conflict. Such a vision is far removed from the usual way in which indigenous peoples in the ancient Near East experienced the advent of invading immigrants and conquering rulers.

The climactic clause of the promise charter in the migration narrative is revealed to Abraham in a theophany after he has traveled deep into Canaanite territory. The specific promise of YHWH is stated quite simply, "To your seed I will give this land" (Gen. 12:7; author's translation). The land promise is thus a discrete doctrine that is announced quite independently and grounded in the charter of a theophany at a local shrine in the midst of the Canaanites. The land promise, which complements the preceding promises of Genesis 12:1-3, is revealed separately in the heartland of Canaan, not in the call event that precedes Abraham's immigration to the host country, according to the migration narratives. The land promise is first given in the land, among the peoples of the land, by the God of the land.

THE LAND COVENANT

The land promise doctrine, launched in the migration narrative, is extended in various ways throughout the Abraham narratives, with explicit speeches from God interrupting the story line. The first such extension is found after Abraham generously offers to share the land and give Lot the richest portion (Gen. 13:5-13). Not only are Abraham and his seed given the land, they can also expect to possess it forever, apparently without condition (13:15).

The eternal character of the land deed is emphasized even more strongly in a subsequent covenant sealed with the rite of circumcision (Gen. 17).[16] Here it is emphasized that the land of Canaan is "an eternal possession" (17:8; author's translation). That the term *'aḥuzzah* ("possession") implies legal ownership is evident from the account of how Abraham buys a plot of land for Sarah's place of burial (23:20; cf. Lev. 25:13, 27). This purchased plot of land is equivalent to a symbolic down payment on Canaan as Israel's legal possession.

Abraham's entitlement to land, based on the promise charters, is offered as an unconditional trust. Here there are none of the conditional clauses typical of the theocratic ideology in Deuteronomy. There are no warnings against being corrupted by Canaanite gods, no requirements to follow the law as a code of behavior, no demand for conditions about care of the land. Abraham's faith in the promise is sufficient evidence of allegiance (Gen. 15:6); performance of the rite of circumcision is sufficient sign of covenant faithfulness (17:9-11, 13).

The charter narrative, which outlines in detail how the land promise is ratified by a treaty, is recorded in Genesis 15:7-21.[17] This land covenant narrative begins with God's self-identification as YHWH, the one involved in bringing Abraham from Ur of the Chaldeans to "possess" the land (Gen. 15:7).[18] Such a message would immediately remind the implied audience of the traditional formula "I am YHWH who brought you from the land of Egypt" (Exod. 20:2; author's translation) and offer an assurance that the seed of Abraham will enjoy the same exodus from Babylon as did their ancestors. Thus the old land and the new land are again linked by the God of the promise.

---

16. Genesis 17 is normally assigned to the Priestly source. For a recent analysis, see Peter von Weimar, "Gen. 17 und die priesterschriftliche Abrahamgeschichte," *ZAW* 100 (1988): 22–60, who considers Genesis 17 central to the Priestly Abraham cycle. Although the emphases are different, this text, like Genesis 15, also ratifies the promise doctrine with a covenant rite.

17. For recent studies on Genesis 15, see E. Haag, "Die Abrahamtradition in Gen. 15," in *Die Vaeter Israels,* edited by A. R. Mueller and M. Görg (Stuttgart: Katholisches Bibelwerk, 1989), 83–106; and J. Scharbert, "Die Landverheissung an die Väter als einfache Zusage, als Eid and als 'Bund,'" in *Konsequente Traditionsgeschichte* (Göttingen: Vandenhoeck & Ruprecht, 1993).

18. Genesis 15:7 is widely recognized as including a reformulation of the formula found in Exodus 20:2. Cf. J. Emerton, "The Origin of the Promises to the Patriarchs in the Older Sources of the Book of Genesis," *VT* 32 (1982): 14–32. Whatever its date, it reflects an ideology that makes the Abraham migration comparable to the exodus migration.

More significantly perhaps, the formula "I am YHWH who brought you from Ur of the Chaldeans, to give you this land to possess" (Gen. 15:7; author's translation), which is clearly modeled on the common formula "I am YHWH who brought you out of the land of Egypt," provides a charter announcement promoting the ideology of the Abraham narratives. By means of this announcement, the migration of Abraham from Ur to Canaan is identified as the work of the same God of Israel and interpreted as comparable with the migration of Israel from Egypt to Canaan. The migration of Abraham is, however, prior to the exodus, and his charter promise is unconditional. The ideology of the Abraham narratives seems, therefore, to be promoting a bond with the land and an entitlement to it that is irrevocable and primary. This tradition of Abraham as the first to take possession of the land may lie behind the land claims of those peasants remaining in the land after the elite are taken into exile; they, as ordinary people like Abraham, assert that they have a right to the land (Ezek. 33:24).

The land treaty narrative presents Abraham, who presumably reflects the mood of the implied audience, as duly skeptical: "How do I know I shall possess it?" (Gen. 15:8; author's translation). The treaty ritual and theophany that follow offer reassurance that entitlement to the land does, in fact, rest in an unconditional charter from the age of Abraham. After Abraham divides the ceremonial animals according to God's direction, a deep and ominous sleep descends on the hero (15:12). This time, the covenant promise is more than a verbal message at a sacred site. The promise of land is intensified by a profound religious experience in the land and an overwhelming theophany by the host deity.

The revealed message associated with this experience refers to a period when Abraham's seed would again immigrate to a land that was not their own (Gen. 15:13). They would, however, return to Canaan when "the iniquity of the Amorites is complete" (15:16; author's translation). This enigmatic expression seeks to explain the delay in taking possession of the land that God has promised. This is the one reference in the Abraham narratives that may perhaps indicate that Abraham's seed will eventually gain the land because of the corruption of the inhabitants (as in Deut. 9:4-5), rather than as a free gift to righteous Abraham. Elsewhere in the Abraham narratives, the emphasis is explicitly on the land as a generous grant and on Abraham as the mediator of blessing to the ancestral families in the land rather than on the inhabitants as evil. Ultimately, Abraham's seed is not expected to get the land by aggression or default, but by virtue of covenant entitlement.

On the awesome day of Abraham's traumatic sleep experience and the mysterious manifestation of God in flame and smoke, YHWH is said to have "cut a covenant with Abraham" (Gen. 15:18; author's translation), guaranteeing the land to Abraham's seed and thereby ratifying the charter of promised land. The covenant event depicted here seems to be a ritual in its own right that has not been modeled on the traditional covenants in Israel, but uses an alternative model from the past. Here Abraham, the progenitor of the people of Israel and the representative of the ancestral households of Israel, is promised the land unconditionally and given control (*yaraš*) over that land for the people.

The territory to be possessed is identified in terms of its ten indigenous inhabitants: the Kenites, the Kenizzites, the Kadmonites, the Hittites, the Perizzites, the Rephaim, the Amorites, the Canaanites, the Girgashites, and the Jebusites (Gen. 15:19-21). This classic list might conjure up memories of the conquest tradition, but no explicit indications are given here that these people are to be expelled or destroyed. On the contrary, the narratives that surround this land covenant suggest that Abraham provided a model of how to live at peace with the host peoples of the land and share ownership of the land. In this ideology, possessing the land does not demand annihilation or expulsion of these peoples. The militant Joshua story is not the logical conclusion of the patriarchal narratives, but an alternative tradition and ideology about possessing the land. The land ideologies of the book of Joshua and the Abraham narratives are apparently in political tension.

LAND RIGHTS AND PEACEFUL RELATIONS

The basic agenda of these land promises is elaborated with artistic subtlety in the narratives of the Abraham saga. Abraham is portrayed as an exemplar of how to share the land, overcome conflict, and mediate blessing to the inhabitants of the land. The host peoples of the land live together with Abraham as a welcome immigrant in their midst. For peaceful relations to be maintained, Abraham must recognize the entitlement of the peoples of Canaan to their respective territories in the land.

When the land chosen by Abraham and Lot cannot support them both and strife arises between their herdsmen, Abraham points to land that is open for settlement, even though the Canaanites seem to be among their neighbors (Gen. 13:1-9). Abraham assumes the right to share the land and magnanimously offers a portion to Lot, who chooses the best territory in the south (13:10). Abraham, the immigrant herdsman, shares the land with Lot (the ancestor of the Moabites and Ammonites) and with the Canaanites of the region. Abraham arrives, it seems, as an agent intent on peaceful coexistence. The land ideology he represents is depicted as accommodating rather than acquisitive.

Abraham's magnanimity in offering to share land and acknowledge Lot's right to land provokes YHWH to reinforce the promise of land to Abraham and his seed. The new version of that promise emphasizes that YHWH's land grant will constitute "all the land" (Gen. 13:14-17). Abraham is invited to walk the length and breadth of the territory in order to chart the territory of the land grant. The ideological implication of this charter account is apparently that by sharing the land and recognizing the rights of the people in the land, Abraham's seed will eventually own the land.

Just as striking is the role Abraham plays in the following narrative, where he and his household of servants take on the invading monarchs who capture Lot. Abraham rescues the household of Lot, the people of Sodom, and the goods confiscated by the invading monarchs and then returns to a royal welcome by the rulers of Sodom and Salem (Gen. 14). Abraham's encounter with each of these monarchs confirms his role as a mediator of goodwill and peaceful relations in Canaan.

Abraham participates in a ritual with Melchizedek, who is not only a king but also a priest from an apparently different religious culture. By so doing, Abraham respects the inhabitants of Salem (presumably the Jebusites); acknowledges their god, El Elyon; receives a blessing from Melchizedek; and responds with a tithe, presumably of his booty (Gen. 14:18-21).

For Abraham to accept a blessing from Melchizedek is to acknowledge his power, his authority as rightful priest of a sacred site in Canaan, and his right to rule the territory of the Jebusites. This acknowledgment of the position of Melchizedek leads to the promotion of peaceful relations with a host people of the land. The immigrant

Abraham is welcomed as a friend in his new host country and culture. As Claus Westermann observes, "Melchizedek brings refreshment to the exhausted liberator and thus as royal host receives him into the peace, the *shalom* of his royal domain."[19]

Here there is no denunciation of Canaanite worship, no condemnation of Canaanite inhabitants, no rejection of Canaanite rulers as oppressors, and no concern about acknowledging a Canaanite deity. The militant ideology of the book of Deuteronomy, which demanded a cleansing of the land of Canaanite religious culture, does not surface in this ideology. Instead, Abraham fosters a way of life in Canaan that mediates blessing and creates peaceful relations with the owners of the land. Abraham, as the head of an ancestral household, here functions as an ambassador of goodwill among equals.

Even the king of the Sodomites is treated with respect. Abraham avoids placing himself in the debt of this king and even swears by the local deity of Salem to emphasize his commitment to sharing rather than exploiting the inhabitants of the land (Gen. 14:21-23). Abraham does not become rich and powerful at the expense of the Canaanites; he does not exploit the indigenous people by keeping the spoils of battle to which he is entitled. Abraham does not play the conqueror. Lives and goods are rescued rather than put to the *herem* of total destruction; the booty is redeemed and returned to its owner. The image of Abraham projected here is of a diplomatic leader respecting the rights of these peoples to their property and their land.

The sequel to this act of goodwill is the effort of Abraham to rescue the city of Sodom from destruction (Gen. 18:16-33). The three men, who had just visited Sarah with the promise of a son, are already on their way to Sodom when YHWH repeats to the implied audience the promise that Abraham would be a great nation, mediate blessing, and instruct his household in the way of justice (18:17-19). As two of the men proceed to Sodom, Abraham stands before YHWH, ready to intercede for the people of Sodom, or, as another ancient reading suggests, YHWH stands before Abraham, the hero of the episode (18:22).

Abraham's intercession on behalf of Sodom demonstrates more than an interest in his relatives in Sodom, who, in fact, are not even men-

19. C. Westermann, *Genesis 12–36* (London: SPCK, 1985), 205.

tioned in this account. Abraham, as the model of righteousness, exhibits a profound concern for justice and the deliverance of what probably became the most notorious city in Canaan. Abraham is the potential mediator of blessing, even to this city. Although nothing could save Sodom, the policy of intercession for Canaanites is indicative of an ideology that promotes justice and goodwill among the host peoples where Abraham's household lives.

The episodes with Abimelech reflect a similar orientation. Contrary to his expectations, Abraham discovers "fear of God" among the Philistines who are found to be a people of integrity (Gen. 20:1-13). These people are not viewed as godless pagans but as neighbors conscious of the divine presence in the land and ready to acknowledge the voice of Abraham's God as the one who appears in dreams.

Abraham's folly in presenting his wife as his sister almost leads to Abimelech's destruction. Only God's intervention prevents the death of Abimelech, who learns from God that Abraham is a prophet capable of interceding for him as he once did for Sodom (Gen. 20:7). In due course, Abimelech sees that the right thing is done by Abraham and exonerates Sarah by bestowing a lavish gift on Abraham (20:14-16). Abimelech could have told Abraham to leave, but instead generously offers Abraham the choice of whatever land he pleases. In a reversal of the story of Abraham sharing land with Lot, it is Abimelech's turn to be magnanimous. Abimelech assumes the right to distribute land to immigrants like Abraham, a right the patriarch does not contest. Abraham lives at peace with the people of Gerar and, surprisingly perhaps, also learns about justice from their ruler. The Philistine culture is remembered in the text as a source of wisdom and truth.

Abimelech is explicitly portrayed as a concerned inhabitant, seeking peace with Abraham. It is Abimelech who has hitherto demonstrated loyalty (*ḥesed*). Now he expects the same kind of just dealings "with me and with the land" where Abraham resides as an immigrant (Gen. 21:22-24). When a dispute arises because the servants of Abimelech have seized a well, Abraham can count on Abimelech's integrity. The resulting treaty guarantees permanent peace between Abraham and these inhabitants of the land and establishes Beer-sheba as a sacred site for Abraham's seed (21:25-34). Peaceful and good relations are cemented by a treaty. With rights to land come responsibilities toward the land and the peoples of the land, even for immigrant aliens.

In these passages, the land and the inhabitants are closely bound. Justice demands that the people and their land are not exploited; this is the justice the inhabitants expect of Abraham as the newcomer. Abimelech asks that Abraham deal fairly with Abimelech and "with the land." Justice for the land presumably means abiding by treaties and respecting the integrity of its peoples. By swearing an oath with the inhabitants before a local deity whom both parties recognize (probably El Olam, Gen. 21:33), Abraham not only respects the Philistines but does justice by the land to which he has migrated and affirms the rights of its owners.

The final episode describing Abraham's dealings with the peoples of the land reflects this same ideological viewpoint (Gen. 23). Sarah dies "in the land of Canaan" (23:2), and Abraham requires a burial place. In spite of his recognized status in the community, he does not assume squatters' rights or take land by force. Rather, he pays the ultimate respect to the Hittites, who are here designated "the people of the land" (23:7). He bows down to them (23:7, 12) and buys the field of Ephron in accordance with the legal procedures depicted as customary among the Hittites. This piece of land then becomes Abraham's permanent legal possession (*ʾaḥuzzah,* 23:18), a symbol of God's promised land and an example of just dealings in the appropriation of land. This legal transaction also implies that Abraham treats the Hittites as the legitimate owners of the land with the right to negotiate its sale.

The Abraham narratives have the hero relating peacefully to a range of inhabitants from diverse cultures. He buys land from the Hittites, attempts to save the Sodomites after rescuing their stolen property, pays tithes to the king of the Jebusites, makes a treaty with the dreaded Philistines, and shares land with Lot, who is his kinsman, the ancestor of the Ammonites and Moabites. Abraham is clearly portrayed as the mediator of peaceful relations and blessing in the land. He is the symbol of an immigrant people seeking to live at peace with the land and building bridges with the existing peoples of the host country, whose rights to the land are thereby acknowledged.

This policy of peace with the peoples of the land recalls the letter of Jeremiah to the exiles in which he urges, "Seek the peace (*šalom*) of the city (LXX: "land") where I have sent you into exile and pray to YHWH on its behalf, for in its peace you will have peace" (Jer. 29:7; author's translation).

Peaceful relations with the indigenous peoples of the host country means peace and prosperity for both Abraham and the host peoples of the land. Possession of land is to be achieved through peaceful means rather than aggressive tactics.

Abraham's power lies in his position as head of the first ancestral household and family of Israel, a position YHWH has chosen to exalt through a charter of promises. In this capacity Abraham recognizes the rights of the peoples of the land, negotiates a share of their land, and mediates peace to the ancestral families of the land. The emphasis on the head of the ancestral household as the locus of authority recalls the social model of Joshua treated in chapter 4. The relationships with the peoples of the land, however, are diametrically opposed. Abraham is depicted as promoting peaceful relations; Joshua is depicted as an advocate of ethnic cleansing.

THE GOD OF THE LAND

At various locations in the host country of Canaan, a deity is revealed to Abraham (Gen. 12:7; 13:14; 15:1; 17:1; 18:1, 22), to Hagar (16:7, 13), and to Abimelech (20:3). This God is associated with several sacred sites and known by a variety of names. The common characteristic of this deity is a close connection with the land. The narrative cycle seems to represent this deity as the God and owner of the land whom the peoples of the land recognize and who assumes the right to promise the land to the new immigrant family of Abraham.

Although there is no explicit statement here that Canaan is "YHWH's land,"[20] as in Leviticus 25:23, or that El is the owner of the land, it is apparent that YHWH is assumed to be the God of the land, the divine landowner, who is located in the land and has the right to bestow the land on Abraham and his seed.[21] YHWH is portrayed as present in the

20. Von Rad, "The Promised Land," 79–93.
21. Wright, 3–23, like other scholars, follows the lead of von Rad and emphasizes YHWH's ownership of the land in the books of Deuteronomy, Leviticus, and elsewhere. Divine ownership in the Abraham cycle, however, is given much less attention by scholars.

land and one with the God revealed at sacred sites within the land. YHWH and the destiny of the anticipated Abraham nation are inextricably bound to this land.

This is not the place to enter the debate about the origins of the names of the God of the ancestors. What is relevant to our discussion here is the portrayal of this deity as part of the ideological perspective of the text. It is clear that this deity is worshiped or recognized by the indigenous peoples of the land. El Elyon, who is identified as "maker [or owner] of heaven and earth" is worshiped by the priest king of Salem, who invokes the blessing of this deity on Abraham (Gen. 14:18-20). Abraham swears by this same God. The immigrant household and the host people gathered at Salem acknowledge the same deity as God at that place.

Abraham also discovers the fear of God among the Philistines, the God whom Abraham identifies as the very one who caused him to leave his ancestral household and immigrate to the land of Canaan (Gen. 20:13). It is precisely this land that the God-fearing Philistines share with the household of Abraham. This God seems to be identical with El Olam, the God whom Abraham recognized in the treaty with the Philistines at Beer-sheba (21:31-33). Abraham acknowledges the presence of this God at Beer-sheba by planting a sacred tree to mark the site as sacred.

The narrator makes it clear, however, that the God of the land, under the various names of El, El Olam, El Elyon, and El Shaddai, is none other than the God who was later revealed as YHWH, the God who liberated the Israelites from slavery. In the circumcision covenant account, which is normally assigned to the Priestly tradition, it is El Shaddai who establishes the covenant (Gen. 17:1-2). Subsequently, according to this tradition, Moses is informed that the God once known to Abraham, Isaac, and Jacob as El Shaddai is none other than YHWH (Exod. 6:2-4). The God who promised the land to the exodus generation of Israelites is the same God who promised the same land in a prior covenant with Abraham.

This god El, under the various designations given in the Abraham narratives, may have connections with the god El found in the Canaanite texts of Ugarit, a deity who seems to be a high god in heaven and the power behind the throne of the storm god, Baal. Admittedly,

God does call out to Abraham from heaven when he attempts to sacrifice his son (Gen. 22:11), but the image of God in the patriarchal narratives is generally not one of a distant celestial high god. Rather, the God of Abraham has intimate conversations with the ancestors, makes personal promises, is revealed as present at specific sites, and invites Abraham's household to share the land. YHWH is revealed to be the God of the peoples and places of the host country to which Abraham immigrates.

The close personal relationship between YHWH and Abraham not only underscores YHWH's close kinship with the land at specific sites but also emphasizes the stature and authority of Abraham as head of the first ancestral household. In this capacity Abraham functions as a priest who, in response to a theophany of YHWH, builds altars and invokes the name of YHWH (Gen. 12:6-8). Abraham is also depicted as a prophet with whom YHWH speaks intimately. At a point outside of Sodom, Abraham, like other prophets, even speaks in the divine council[22] on behalf of the inhabitants of Sodom (18:16, 22). YHWH, as the God of the land, talks repeatedly with the new immigrants, dines with Abraham and Sarah, and blesses their interaction with the peoples of the land.[23]

SUMMARY

The land of Canaan is presented as a host country inhabited by a range of peoples whose rights and cultures Abraham respects. These rights include their right to own, share, sell, and negotiate the use of land in the host country. The land is also portrayed as charted terrain, marked by the journeys of the ancestors and the sacred sites they established at strategic points in the host country.

The doctrine of the land, as promised to the ancestors, is elaborated in a series of charter narratives that underscore the unconditional nature of the ancestral entitlement to land, ratification of the promise by theophany and treaty, the correlative promise of progeny to possess all the

---

22. Van Seters, *Prologue to History,* 259, points out that the "purpose of the visitation is to make Abraham a party to the deliberations of the divine council."
23. Although this chapter has been confined to an analysis of the Abraham cycle of narratives, there are indications of a similar ideology in parts of the Jacob cycle, especially Genesis 32–34. See Brueggemann, *The Land.*

land, and the symbolic anticipation of possessing land by the purchase of property for Sarah's burial. Implied in these ideological charter narratives seems to be the priority of the unconditional promise of land to the patriarchs over the conditional promise to the exodus generation of Israelites.

God, who is revealed to Abraham and promises him land, is present at specific sites in the land to which Abraham migrates. This God is identified as both El, the God worshiped under various names by the peoples of the land, and as YHWH, the God who effected the exodus of Abraham from Ur long before the exodus of Israel from Egypt. This God, as owner of the land, assumes the right to promise it to Abraham, Sarah, and their progeny.

The herdsman Abraham and his extensive household, including his wife, Sarah, and nephew, Lot, are portrayed as immigrants to the host country of Canaan. As an immigrant, Abraham shares the land either through generous grants, peaceful negotiations, or legal purchase. Abraham's power is not exhibited in military might, but in the mediation of blessing and the establishment of peaceful relations. As an immigrant group, Abraham's household will be good for the country. The blessing power associated with royalty is democratized and vested in Abraham as the head of an ancestral household.

The ideology of the Abraham cycle has Abraham formally recognizing the rights of the host peoples to their various territories. This recognition is established through cultic rites, peaceful negotiation, treaty, and land purchase. Abraham's short-term right to land is that of a welcome immigrant, not an invader. In the long term, Abraham's entitlement is grounded in a land treaty announced by YHWH. Abraham's rights and responsibilities are not those of a monarch or conqueror, but those of the head of an ancestral household. These responsibilities involve acknowledging YHWH as the host deity, teaching justice to the Abraham household, establishing peaceful relations with the peoples of the land, and dealing justly with the land itself.

CHAPTER 8

Comparisons, Conclusions, and Implications

The preceding chapters offer a discussion of six biblical ideologies based on several broad categories of analysis: the dominant image of land, the location of God, charters of entitlement, and the locus of power and rights to or of the land. To appreciate the distinctive features of each ideology, it is helpful to provide a summary comparison of the key elements included in each of these ideologies, using the preceding categories of analysis as a basic guide.

Our comparison focuses first on the central or dominant image of the land, which serves as an integrating doctrine in each of the complex schemas of ideas promoted in the respective ideologies. Although some analysts may quibble about the precise details of the following formulation, these images represent a bold profile suitable for highlighting the similarities and differences between these ideologies.

DOMINANT IMAGES OF THE LAND

The six dominant images of the land, which function as doctrines central to the respective ideologies, can be summarized as follows:

In the royal ideology, land is a source of centralized wealth and glory for the monarch and the empire, the monarch being the earthly representative of YHWH located in heaven; the people are the monarch's labor force in the land.

In the theocratic ideology of the book of Deuteronomy, Canaan is a land grant, an unearned gift from YHWH, its owner and custodian; the people of Israel have conditional entitlement to the land by treaty.

134

In the ancestral household ideology of the book of Joshua, land is a cluster of promised entitlements in Canaan allotted by YHWH to ancestral households who are to undertake the conquest and settlement of their allotments.

In the prophetic ideology of the book of Jeremiah, land is YHWH's own pure and precious *naḥalah;* the land suffers great anguish when defiled by the people who YHWH has chosen to plant in the land; the landowner, YHWH, suffers with the land.

In the agrarian ideology in the book of Leviticus 25–27, land is YHWH's personal sanctuary and garden, worked by Israelite families as tenant farmers on their traditional properties, and bound by the principles of a sabbath economy.

In the immigrant ideology of the Abraham narratives, land is a host country where immigrant ancestors find God at sacred sites, discern promises of future land, and establish peaceful relations with the indigenous peoples of the land.

In most of these ideologies, the land of Canaan is depicted in appealing material terms as good, pleasant, and fertile, replete with grain fields, vineyards, and olive orchards. The distinctive images of the land in each of the ideologies summarized here go beyond these physical portraits to indicate the social and political relationships among YHWH, the land, and the people of the land.

The royal ideology, which views land as a source of wealth and status for the monarch and the empire, is more interested in fortress cities, administrative districts, and revenue centers than the ancestral plots with which peasants may have bonded. The royal texts project an image of distance between the royal seat of power and the land as its source of wealth. The people of the land are the labor force and the means by which the monarch accumulates wealth and glory. The land may extend beyond the traditional boundaries of Canaan to include conquered territories and ultimately the whole inhabited earth. As the representative of YHWH, who is the monarch over heaven and earth, the earthly monarch's empire potentially extends to the ends of the earth. The monarch has the capacity to acquire ancestral plots in order to expand the royal estates or to distribute them to favored officials.

The act of YHWH giving the land of Canaan to Israel, in the theocratic ideology of Deuteronomy, really means granting Israel legal entitlement to ownership of that land. Canaan is a land grant from YHWH, the owner of all lands. The doctrine of gift that reinforces this grant promotes a sense of total dependency on YHWH as the magnanimous giver. The Israelites are reminded forcefully and repeatedly that they do not earn or deserve the land. The technical term for Israel's entitlement to this land is *naḥalah.* Israel receives the land as an undeserved allotment from YHWH, the owner of the land. Grateful acceptance of this entitlement also involves cleansing the land of the existing Canaanite occupants.

In the ideology of the book of Joshua, the territories allotted for distribution are identified as the royal lands of Canaanite kings, to be transferred to the ancestral families of the people of Israel. Each ancestral family and household is to receive its own *naḥalah,* its allotted entitlement from this legacy of royal lands. Although these allotments are legally recognized, initiative is required to clear the indigenous inhabitants and settle the claimed allotments.

The book of Jeremiah, while recognizing the land as Israel's *naḥalah,* moves the spotlight to the land as YHWH's personal *naḥalah.* As YHWH's own plot of land, Canaan is virgin and pure. When Israel pollutes the land, the land responds as an injured victim. The land is depicted as a person in pain; YHWH threatens to empty this *naḥalah* of all its pollutants.

Interestingly, the agrarian ideology in the text of Leviticus 25–27, while focusing on the return of family lands in the year of jubilee, avoids the term *naḥalah* and refers instead to each farmer's plot of land as *ʾaḥuzzah,* personal property. The land, which YHWH owns, is an extended sanctuary and garden on which farmers function as tenants, each with their own *ʾaḥuzzah.* The land as a whole and all its tenant holdings are bound by a sabbath economy that demands that all YHWH's lands have rest from all agriculture every seven years and every fiftieth year.

The image of the land of Canaan in the immigrant ideology of the Abraham narratives is markedly different. The land is an expansive host country in which Canaanites, Hittites, Philistines, and a range of other peoples live; Abraham establishes peaceful relations with the host peoples of the land. The land is also a sacred map on which are charted the trails of the ancestors and the sacred sites where the El, the God of the land, is revealed. The ideology is also careful to identify this God as YHWH, who became known as the God of Israel.

LOCATION AND FUNCTION OF GOD

Potentially, the image of God in relation to the land could range from that of a remote high god, who once created the earth, retired to heaven, and then operated as the power behind the scenes, to that of an earth god, who is virtually identical with the land and its vibrant, creative forces. Between these two poles a wide range of options is possible. Within the land ideologies analyzed in the preceding chapters, God is always a powerful being quite distinct from the stuff of earth. The spatial imagery employed to describe the locus of God is, however, an indicator of the relationship of God to the land and integral to a given ideology.

At one end of the spectrum, God, as the creator of the cosmos and the one who has established the cosmic order, chooses to make heaven a dwelling place and base of operations. God intervenes from above through an earthly ruler who represents God on earth or, more specifically, in the land of God's people. In the royal ideology, the monarch rules the land below on behalf of YHWH, who is monarch of the cosmos above. The monarch's cry is that YHWH would "hear in heaven your dwelling place" and intervene on behalf "of your servant and of your people" (1 Kings 8:30). Even when distraught penitents pray "toward their land" or God's house, it is from heaven that God hears and acts (8:48-49).

In the ideologies in the books of Deuteronomy and Joshua, YHWH claims to be the owner of both heaven and earth, ruling all lands and controlling events from on high. YHWH's lordship over the earth, made evident in the rescue of the Israelites from Egypt, is to be demonstrated publicly by using celestial might to subdue the Promised Land and empty it of all unwanted inhabitants. This military might is aggressively displayed in the conquest narratives of Joshua, who, with the help of the commander of YHWH's celestial army, leads the Israelite invasion of Canaan.

These three ideologies reflect a strong hierarchical model of God's relationship to land reminiscent of the paradigm found in Genesis 1. In that mythic charter, God creates and rules by decree, establishing the sun and moon to "rule" in the sky above and human beings to "rule" the land below and "subdue" it. The ideological emphasis lies on the likeness between God and humans as rulers, rather than on a close kinship between humans and the earth they are expected to subdue.

In the ideology of the book of Jeremiah, YHWH is acknowledged as creator of the cosmic order, but the dominant image is that of YHWH as the source of fertility relishing the dispersal of generous blessings upon the chosen land. YHWH upstages even Baal by assuming the title *ba'al*, ruler of the earth. More important, YHWH expresses a deep affinity and personal sympathy with the land; YHWH speaks directly to the land and suffers anguish over its desolation. YHWH's ties are primarily with the land itself rather than with any abode on the land or in the sky.

A similar sense of kinship with the land is found in the agrarian ideology of Leviticus 25–27. In this vision of agrarian society, YHWH is not an absentee landowner ruling or managing farms from heaven, but a local landowner who resides in the land and walks through the land as a personal garden. YHWH's continuous presence in the land of Canaan is depicted in terms reminiscent of God's primordial presence in the Garden of Eden. The land is the chosen abode of YHWH as the divine farmer par excellence.

All of these ideologies depict YHWH as the source of abundant fertility, whether it be as the monarch of heaven sending rain from on high, the *ba'al* of the land fertilizing personal property, or the God of the garden producing a bumper harvest every six years. The agrarian and prophetic ideologies seem to reflect a particular belief that fertilizing the land of Canaan is something personal and integral to the function of YHWH. YHWH not only owns the land but also is involved in actively tending the land.

The location and image of God in relation to the land, found in the immigrant ideology of the Abraham narratives, differs significantly from the patterns found in the preceding ideologies. The emphasis is not on the fertility of farmlands; Abraham is depicted as a herdsman, not a farmer. Farming in the patriarchal tradition begins only with Isaac, who sows seed in the land and reaps a hundredfold (Gen. 26:12). Abraham locates his God at various points in the land as he travels through it with extensive herds of sheep, cattle, donkeys, and camels. This God blesses Abraham's herds and household.

The locations in the land where this God is revealed to Abraham are remembered by the Israelite people as important sacred sites. The God who is revealed at these sites is El, variously designated as El, El Elyon, El Shaddai, and El Olam, and worshiped by the peoples in the land. This god is recognized in the narrative as identical with YHWH, the God of Israel (Exod. 6:2, 3). This God, who in one text is designated "El Elyon, maker [or owner] of heaven and earth" (Gen. 14:19), claims ownership of the land and the right to deed it over permanently to the seed of Abraham. The localizing of God in the land and in sacred sites of the land stands in direct contrast with the high-god orientation of the royal and theocratic ideologies.

CHARTERS JUSTIFYING ENTITLEMENT

The doctrine of YHWH promising the land of Canaan as a gift to the ancestors provides a justification for Israel's entitlement to the land in all six of the ideologies discussed here (1 Kings 8:48; Deut. 1:8; Josh. 1:6; Jer. 16:15; Lev. 26:42; Gen 15:18). The land of Canaan is, above all, the land claimed by the Israelites as their legitimate and legal entitlement because of the promise of YHWH, which is confirmed by revelation to the ancestors and ratified by treaty. This doctrine is promulgated as assured, even where the identity of the ancestors is a matter of debate.

The Genesis narratives include a range of charter narratives recording several accounts and occasions when this land promise was revealed to the first ancestors and their seed. Entitlement to the land is sealed as a legal charter in the land treaty made between Abraham and YHWH (Gen. 15). In a variant of this treaty, permanent ownership of the land is promised by El Shaddai (17:8). The land promise is the enduring doctrine to which the Israelites appeal in subsequent crises when their fate on the land is in the balance.

The theocratic ideology of Deuteronomy contends, however, that this charter is not irrevocable. Faithlessness to YHWH and to YHWH's law for life on the land can mean that Israel is "destroyed from the face of the land" (Deut. 6:15; author's translation). The ideology in the book of

Joshua reflects a similar perspective (Josh. 24:19-20), whereas the text of Jeremiah anticipates the end of the old treaty (Jer. 31:31-32).

All of the ideologies, except the immigrant ideology, anticipate that the people of Israel will go into exile and leave the promised land empty. The grounds for this negation of the original charter, however, vary in accordance with the principles of the ideology involved. In the royal ideology, the rationale given is simply a sin against YHWH in heaven that evokes celestial anger (1 Kings 8:46-50; cf. 8:35-36). In the books of Deuteronomy and Joshua, loss of land is threatened if the Israelites do not annihilate the Canaanites, showing them no pity; Israel is also required by treaty to remain faithful to YHWH's law for the land, to avoid intermarriage with Canaanites, and to shun contact with their gods (Deut. 7:1-6, 12-16; Josh. 23:13). This isolationist policy is promulgated as essential to survival on the land.

In line with the virgin land ideology of the book of Jeremiah, loss of land is caused by defilement of YHWH's personal *nahalah;* the land must be purged and emptied before a new planting can begin. The agrarian ideology in the text of Leviticus 25–27 anticipates land loss if Israel does not uphold the sabbath economy enunciated in the law code. Israel must lose the land to gain it; in losing the land, the promises and the demands of YHWH, the landowner, are finally valued.

It could be argued that this common theme of land loss and exile points to an exilic context as the historical circumstance for the promotion of these ideologies, or at least for the final form of their literary production. It might be worth exploring, however, whether, in view of Israel's political history, land loss was incorporated as a typical feature of coherent land ideologies grounded in a theology of YHWH as the jealous landowner who expects land grants to be appreciated.

The image of the land as empty and devoid of inhabitants (*terra nullius*) seems to justify the claim of returning exiles that their lands have no other rightful owners or occupants. The exiles are led to believe that they can return to their ancestral entitlements. God has cleared and cleaned the land for the Israelites to occupy afresh without any legitimate opposition. The myth of the empty land is thereby perpetuated.

In addition to remembering the common doctrine of land promised to ancestors, these ideologies incorporate complementary charters that reinforce and/or reinterpret the original land doctrine. The relative force of these supplementary charters varies from schema to schema.

The doctrine that orients the royal ideology is the election of the monarch as YHWH's son and the promised allocation of the earth and its nations as the monarch's *nahalah*. The land of Canaan, represented by its capital, thus becomes the administrative and religious center of the empire. The land of the monarch's dominion extends beyond the land given to the people as their *nahalah*.

The charter narrative that justifies the monarch's right to wealth and, consequently, to the land as the source of this wealth is enunciated in Solomon's dream vision at Gibeon. His astute request for wisdom results in a declaration of his right to wealth and glory. This declaration is tantamount to an alternative promise that grounds the right of the monarchs to assume ownership of the land promised to Israel and to dispense of it as they choose.

The charter events that provide the rationale for underscoring the gift doctrine promoted in the book of Deuteronomy are the deliverance of the Israelites from Egypt and the revelation on Mount Sinai of YHWH's law for the land. When Israel enjoys the land promised to the ancestors, they are not to forget the God of the exodus who made their settlement possible (Deut. 6:10-12, 20-23); they are to keep the law for the land, given at Sinai (5:2), confirmed in Moab (28:69 in Hebrew), and to be inscribed on large stones set up in the land during the land grant ceremony (27:1-3).

The limited conquest campaigns in the book of Joshua are promulgated as evidence that the promises of land made to the ancestors and repeated to Moses were fulfilled. The doctrine of fulfilled promises seems to be promoted not only as a justification for Israel's claim to the land as a *nahalah* (Josh. 11:23), but also as a vision and challenge for ancestral households to follow the lead of Joshua and possess their individual entitlements. The initiatives of ancestral households like that of Caleb are included as narratives that reinforce the Joshua model.

The ideology of the book of Jeremiah does not simply assume or assert YHWH's ownership of the land, as do the ideologies of the texts of Deuteronomy, Joshua, and Leviticus 25-27. Rather, the book of Jeremiah seems to ground YHWH's relationship with the land in an ancient mythic charter (Deut. 32:8-9), according to which each of the nations were allotted a land as a *naḥalah*. YHWH's land is declared to be "the most beautiful *naḥalah* of all the nations" (Jer. 3:19; cf. 10:16; 12:10), the *naḥalah* in which YHWH planted the people of Israel.

The agrarian ideology in the text of Leviticus 25–27 bases the sabbath economy, incumbent upon the people who are given the land, on a direct mandate from Moses "on Mount Sinai" (Lev. 25:1-2; 26:46; 27:34). YHWH's ownership of the farming land of Canaan is based on a declaration that "the land is mine" (25:23) and that all the people are alien tenants.

The repeated promise of land in the Abraham narratives is also reinforced by a number of related charter narratives. Abraham's purchase of the cave of Machpelah, as the burial site for Sarah, functions as a charter story promising future land as a permanent possession of Abraham's seed. Interestingly, the land travel and land promise narratives stand in tension with the stories about the promise of a son. Abraham gets a true son and heir only after numerous false starts and failures; the promise of land is an unconditional charter. Without a son, however, there can be no future ancestral family to receive land as an entitlement from God.

THE LOCUS OF POWER AND RIGHTS TO THE LAND

The locus of power in the land and the rights of groups to land are interrelated categories of analysis that are treated together in this comparative summary. Those who claim or aspire to power, and whose vested interests are reflected in a given biblical ideology, tend to be those who claim the right to own or control land. This claim raises the question of justice for groups who are excluded from land entitlement.

A distinction needs to be made between Israel's right to the land of Canaan as a whole and the rights of groups or individuals to land within or beyond Canaan. The charters and doctrines that justify Israel's right to possess the land of Canaan as a promise, edict, gift, and conquest of YHWH have been discussed and need not be elaborated further.

Who are the groups using these doctrines to promote their interests in rights to land in Canaan at the time indicated in the text, whether that be the present or the future for the implied audience? Are there implied counterclaims by those groups who represent opposing or oppressed groups in the same society?

We may assume, as a starting point, that most of these land ideologies are being promoted by particular landholders or would-be landholders.

We may also assume that the texts under discussion are the product of those with vested interests in gaining or maintaining control of land. These assumptions, of course, need to be tested by analyzing each ideology in its social complexity.

It also needs to be recognized that the doctrine of YHWH's promise of Canaan, which justifies Israel's entitlement to the land and which is common to all six ideologies, is not a theological axiom that stands alone. Rather, this doctrine is appropriated and adapted by specific power groups who use it to promote their claims for control or ownership of all or parts of the land.

The interests vested in the royal ideology are clearly located in the monarch who claims not only the right to own extensive personal estates but also the right to control all the land of Canaan and potentially all other lands as well. This power of the monarch is shared with those officials who gain royal favor and enjoy largesse. Even though the Deuteronomic framework of the royal ideology document, preserved in 1 Kings 3–10, is critical of the monarch's religious misdeeds and marriage alliances (e.g., 1 Kings 11), this document stands as a testimony to those royalists who promoted the Solomonic ideal as the symbol of royal ideology. The promotion of this ideology seems to be at the expense of the priests, whose power and status are reduced to being listed among the other officials of the imperial administration (4:1-6).

In spite of a prophetic tradition critical of the royal ideology, the monarch could claim the right to take and dispense the best lands of Israelite peasants and conquered peoples. In the monarch's pursuit of glory for the empire, disenfranchised Canaanites, conquered peoples, and even ordinary Israelites could be subjected to corvée labor. The monarch assumed absolute power over land allotments and claimed this power as a divine right.

The locus of power in the theocratic ideal in the book of Deuteronomy is with the Levites and, in particular, with the Levitical priests who have YHWH rather than land as their personal *nahalah*. They are entitled to cities rather than farms as their property in YHWH's land. The Levites' power is established by virtue of their control over the covenant law, which governs polity and survival for Israel in the land. This law is intended to restrict the powers of all social groups, including prophets, judges, and monarchs, and to give the

Levites pride of place. The Levites are promoted as the guardians of the law books and the interpreters of the *lex terrae.*

Individual land allotments seem to be controlled by ancestral households, although their entitlement to the particular allotments is implied rather than made explicit. The boundaries of these allotments were sacrosanct. These households included slaves and laborers who had no rights to land as such but were theoretically protected by the justice of covenant law. The produce of the land was to be shared with the poor, widows, orphans, and strangers in the land, all of whom were totally disenfranchised in terms of land claims.

The ideology in the book of Joshua promotes the status, rights, and responsibilities of ancestral households and their heads. Traditional ancestral families claimed the right to territories that were allotted to them by YHWH, who directed the lots apportioned by Joshua in the distribution of Canaanite lands. The heads of ancestral households within these extended families are urged to follow the model of Joshua, whose household took the initiative in choosing YHWH and claiming land. The heads of these households are strongly urged to exercise their power and claim the land that is rightfully theirs.

By promoting the Joshua model of power located with the heads of ancestral households, this ideology counters the doctrine of a centralized royal or priestly model of leadership. Even in the case of the Levites, it is the heads of the ancestral families who press the claim for, and presumably control, the towns and pasture lands they are allotted throughout the land. The priests and Levites play a role in the cultic realm, but it is Joshua, the household head par excellence, who demands total allegiance to YHWH in the final showdown of Joshua 24.

In the book of Jeremiah, the prophet challenges the power of prophets, priests, and rulers in the land because they do not "know YHWH" as the true lord of the land and ultimate source of power. In the future age envisaged in the text of Jeremiah, all God's people, from the least to the greatest, will know YHWH. Future rulers will be informed by the same knowledge and consequently will govern with genuine justice.

In this ideology, rights to land, however, are concentrated with the elite who experienced loss of land by going into exile. After the destruction of Jerusalem by the Babylonians, the land is to be emptied of the peasant poor left behind in the land, who forfeited their right to land by disobeying God and fleeing to Egypt. Jeremiah's redemption of land belonging to his family entitlement points to a future when ancestral families will again enjoy their land rights. In this ideology there is, however, no persistent push for the landless poor, as distinct from the landless elite in exile, to be granted land, in spite of YHWH's initial offer to the peasants (Jer. 42:10-12).

In the proposed rural economy in the text of Leviticus 25–27, urban elite landowners, who controlled peasant lands throughout much of Israel's history, are explicitly excluded from authority over, or rights to, the properties of established peasant farmers. Individual peasant farmers have a perpetual right to their traditional lands as their legally owned property (ʾaḥuzzah). This right extended to the redemption of lost lands in good times and their complete restoration in the year of jubilee. The principle of restoration applied only to the lands of established peasant farmers.

Although the right to own land rested primarily with the privileged peasant farmers, the priests, who had authority over the administration of the sabbath economy, could, over time, accumulate land and the social power associated with land ownership. Land, deeded to priests by a vow of consecration to YHWH, could become their permanent possession. The landless poor, farm laborers, slaves, and resident aliens, however, had no right to own land permanently. The particular priests who promoted this agrarian economy seem to have upheld the rights of the peasant farmers over those of the urban elite as a way of establishing a rural power base rather than a centralized one for their priesthood.

From the perspective of the invading Israelites, the various peoples of Canaan, here designated as the Canaanites, can be considered the indigenous peoples of the land. In none of the ideologies, except the immigrant ideology, is their right to occupy or possess land given serious consideration. These indigenous peoples are variously portrayed as the enemy, the unbelievers, or the unclean occupants of the land. As such, they are destined to be dispossessed and destroyed. According to these ideologies, those who survive can expect only to be slaves, even though several texts recognize that this did not always happen in reality (Josh. 15:63). The notable exceptions to this portrait are Caleb and

Rahab, whose allegiance to God and the cause of Moses was so total that they could be considered genuine Israelites at heart.

The immigrant ideology of the Abraham narratives has a totally different perspective on land entitlement in relation to the Canaanites. The locus of political power lies with the Canaanite peoples who share their land with the immigrant family of Abraham. They are the host peoples, and Canaan is the host country. In none of Abraham's dealings with these peoples is their right to possess the land in question. Nor are they, as a totality, regularly depicted as enemies or unbelievers who deserve to be expunged from the land. Abraham even tries to rescue the sinful Sodomites and pays a tithe to the priest-king of Salem.

Abraham respects the Canaanites, their culture, their god, and their territories. Where land is in dispute, he negotiates peaceful settlements. When the land is attacked, he fights for the peoples of the land. When he needs a burial site for Sarah, he buys land in accordance with the local laws of land purchase. Abraham is a peaceful immigrant who willingly recognizes the land entitlements of the peoples of the host country.

Even the promises to Abraham about future possession of the land focus on Abraham mediating blessing to other families of the land, rather than on the annihilation of his hosts. In these narratives the peoples of the land are blessed through contact with Abraham. Melchizedek, in turn, calls down the blessing of El Elyon, the god of Salem, upon Abraham. Thus Abraham, the head of the first ancestral household and family, becomes a model of responsible power in peaceful negotiations and legal acquisition of land.

The ideologies of power, reflected in the images of Abraham and Joshua as heads of ancestral households, are in sharp conflict with each other. Joshua and his household reject all the gods of Canaan, choose YHWH alone, call for a ban to annihilate all Canaanites, and take over all their material culture as booty either for God or for themselves. According to the ideology of the Abraham narrative, the patriarch respects El, the creator God of Canaan, identifies El with YHWH, mediates material blessings to the Canaanites, and negotiates a peaceful sharing of the land.

As indicated earlier, these land ideologies, quite understandably, are generally written from the perspective of the landowners or would-be landowners, whether they be monarchs, priests, peasant farmers, or heads of ancestral families. If, however, they were written from the perspective of the landless poor or dispossessed Canaanites, they would present a very different interpretation of the images, doctrines, and charters of these ideologies.

The only ideology that reflects any sympathy for the indigenous Canaanites is the immigrant ideology of the Abraham narratives. Under this ideology, the Canaanites could at least expect to be blessed, rather than cursed, through the seed of Abraham.

RIGHTS OF THE LAND

Do any of these ideologies go beyond the rights of YHWH as landowner, the rights of Israel as a people to occupy land, or the rights of particular social groups or individuals to control portions of land? Do any of these ideologies consider the rights of the land itself, even indirectly?

It might be argued that this is a contemporary environmental question that has no place in a consideration of biblical land ideologies. It might also be expected that where ideologies are concerned about promoting the rights of a people or a class of society, the rights of the land as such would not be raised. A further examination of these ideologies, however, reveals several factors relevant to this question.

In the agrarian ideology of the text of Leviticus 25–27, the land itself is bound by the sabbath principle. It is not only YHWH, the landowner, or YHWH's tenants who are obliged to rest every seven years, but the arable land is also expected to enjoy its sabbaths (Lev. 25:5). The land, it seems, has a right to be free of those agricultural activities that demand produce from the soil; YHWH's garden is not to be exploited by continuous or increased productivity. Violation of this sabbath principle by the tenants will result in YHWH emptying the land of people in order to grant it enforced rest. The rights of the land are thus to be secured by divine mandate.

The royal and theocratic ideologies, which locate God in heaven, tend to ignore the rights and feelings of the land. In these ideologies there is not the same strong sense of kinship between God and the ground as in the agrarian ideology of Leviticus 25–27 and the prophetic ideology of the book of Jeremiah. In the ideologies of the books of Joshua and Deuteronomy, in spite of the glowing descriptions of the land and its produce, the land is not depicted as sensitive to acts of conquest or settlement. In these ideologies it is YHWH's blessing from above that is hailed as primary.

The prophetic ideology of the book of Jeremiah, however, promotes a close, symbiotic relationship between Israel, YHWH, and the land. As YHWH's *nahalah,* the land is more than just another possession. The land responds to the way it is treated as if it were a highly sensitive partner of both YHWH and Israel. When the land is violated by religious and social pollution, the land suffers, mourns, and cries out in anguish. The anguish of the land is one with that of YHWH and Jeremiah. The land is not a passive object but an active partner living in a close relationship with the people who dwell on this soil.

The rights of the land are not mentioned specifically in the immigrant ideology of the Abraham narratives, but the respect shown for the culture of the Canaanites suggests a respect for the land. One example of this respect is found in the treaty between Abimelech and Abraham, in which Abimelech insists that Abraham deal justly "with me and with the land where you are an immigrant" (Gen. 21:23; author's translation). Abraham is asked to show loyalty to the land in the same way that Abimelech has done. The land, too, is a party to the treaty relationship established with the people of the land.

IMPLICATIONS

It is not within the parameters of this book to draw out the implications of this study for the various land and land rights issues being debated in political and religious circles in the twentieth century. I hope that these studies in the land ideologies of the Hebrew Scriptures will provide resources that can be used by those interested in biblical materials and that may contribute to the resolution of these issues.

Whether or not particular scholars agree with the detailed analyses of particular ideologies treated in this book, these studies make it abundantly clear that there is no monolithic concept of land in the Hebrew Scriptures. There is, rather, a spectrum of land ideologies with diverse images and doctrines of land. These ideologies, moreover, are promoted by particular social groups with vested interests in promoting a given ideology to gain, regain, or maintain land.

Land Ideology
Classification Grid

	ROYAL IDEOLOGY 1 KINGS 3–10, ROYAL PSALMS	THEOCRATIC IDEOLOGY DEUTERONOMY
A: DOMINANT IMAGES OF THE LAND What dominant images, concepts, metaphors, and terms are used to depict the land, convey a particular orientation to the land, and thereby help to promote a given ideology?	Land as • Source of royal wealth and power • Royal estates and revenue centers • Domain given for royal rule by God • Empire embracing all earth	Land as • An undeserved gift and legal possession from YHWH • Filled with towns, crops, herds, and so on for Israel • A gift conditional upon clearing out its inhabitants • Good, fertile habitation prepared by the Canaanites
B: LOCATION OF GOD What is the location of God in the cosmic scheme of things? What is God's position relative to the earth, the land, and the people in the land? What metaphors dominate this relationship? What is God's relative kinship with the land?	YHWH • Monarch ruling from high above • Founder of cosmic order • Dwelling place in heaven • Source of blessing and justice for earth	YHWH • Universal monarch, ruler over all lands • Landowner who controls events from on high • Rescues Israel from slavery to reveal universal rule • Demonstrates dominion by mighty deeds in Canaan • Source of fertility and order in land

C: CHARTERS JUSTIFYING ENTITLEMENT TO LAND On what grounds do Israel or certain individuals or groups justify claiming entitlement to land? What stories, divine edicts, or traditions function as charters for the ideology being espoused?	The promise • Of land made to ancestors • Of wealth to rule in dream vision • To David of a son to be temple builder Edict • Declaring monarch to be God's son • Declaring earth the monarch's *naḥalah*	The promise • Of the land made to the ancestors • Confirmed as a mandate from YHWH to Moses • Assured by YHWH's will to clear the land of peoples A law code • Designed to enable long life in the land • To be ratified in a land grant ceremony
D. LOCUS OF POWER IN THE LAND Where is the locus of power in the social order projected within the ideology? Whose interests are being served by the endorsement of this ideology? How is the locus of power linked to the land?	With the monarch who • Controls all the land and rules for YHWH • Mediates wealth through wisdom • Mediates fertility to the land • Is God's chosen son • Assumes authority over the priests	The power • Of YHWH as head of the theocracy and owner of the land • Of elders, judges, and even monarchs is restricted • Over the law in the theocracy rests with the Levites • Of the Levites is grounded in YHWH as their *naḥalah*

E. RIGHTS TO OR OF THE LAND		
What rights do the people, particular groups of people, or individuals have to the land? Are these rights understood in terms of justice? Are any groups excluded? Is the land itself viewed as having any rights or entitlements?	**The people** • Have a right to the land, but. . . . • Become monarch's labor force • Are like the poor, who have no rights **The monarch** • Assumes a right to rule the land • Has the right to take the land he chooses • Claims a right to rule the earth **The land** • Itself has no rights	**Israel** • Has a God-given right, not a natural right to the land • Forfeits rights if the people violate the law for the land • Forfeits rights if the people forget who gave them land **The Levites** • Have YHWH, not land, as their entitlement **Ancestral households** • Have land entitlements, but the poor and the laborer are denied rights to the land **The Canaanites** • Are the enemy and without rights **The land** • Although tended by YHWH is not accorded rights

	ANCESTRAL HOUSEHOLD IDEOLOGY JOSHUA	PROPHETIC IDEOLOGY JEREMIAH
A: DOMINANT IMAGES OF THE LAND What dominant images, concepts, metaphors, and terms are used to depict the land, convey a particular orientation to the land, and thereby help to promote a given ideology?	Land as • The domain promised to the ancestors • Conquered royal lands of Canaan • A cluster of family lots in Canaan • An entitlement (*naḥalah*) for each ancestral family • Lots still to be taken and settled	Land as • YHWH's *naḥalah*, a personal allotment • Israel's *naḥalah*, an allotment from YHWH • A pure, fertile plot for planting YHWH's people • Polluted by fertility rites and the like • Personified victim suffering from evils • Space to remain empty until after the exile
B: LOCATION OF GOD What is the location of God in the cosmic scheme of things? What is God's position relative to the earth, the land, and the people in the land? What metaphors dominate this relationship? What is God's relative kinship with the land?	YHWH • Ruler in heaven above • Owner and distributor of lands • Renowned warrior who fights from heaven • Jealous God who destroys the Canaanites	YHWH • Ruler of heaven and earth • Source of fertility over personal land • *baʿal*, jealous custodian of land • Closely bonded with personal land • In anguish over its pollution and desolation

| C: CHARTERS JUSTIFYING ENTITLEMENT TO LAND On what grounds do Israel or certain individuals or groups justify claiming entitlement to land? What stories, divine edicts, or traditions function as charters for the ideology being espoused? | The promise
• Of land made to the ancestors

The mandate
• From Moses to possess the land

The narratives
• Of Joshua's fulfilling the promise
• Of initiatives taken to claim unconquered lands
• Of Joshua, the model of "choosing YHWH" alone | Story of
• YHWH bringing Israel as bride to virgin land
• YHWH giving a *naḥalah* to a beautiful bride
• YHWH planting Israel in a personal *naḥalah*

Promise of
• YHWH replanting the people after the exile
• Future land claims symbolized by Jeremiah's redemption of his ancestral land |
| D: LOCUS OF POWER IN THE LAND Where is the locus of power in the social order projected within the ideology? Whose interests are being served by the endorsement of this ideology? How is the locus of power linked to the land? | Power is
• Vested in Joshua by Moses
• Exhibited by Joshua in military conquest
• Located in Joshua's role as ideal head of ancestral household (*bet ʾab*)
• Not in Joshua as model of the royal ideal
• Vested in the heads of ancestral households
• Also found in priests as heads under Joshua | Power is
• True power in "knowing YHWH"
• Prophets, priests, and monarchs do not "know YHWH"
• Power accorded Babylon to empty the land
• All God's people will know YHWH in new age
• Just monarchs will feed people with this knowledge |

| E. RIGHTS TO OR OF THE LAND

What rights do the people, particular groups of people, or individuals have to the land? Are these rights understood in terms of justice? Are any groups excluded? Is the land itself viewed as having any rights or entitlements? | Right to land
• Is granted to ancestral families and households
• Is based on the lots distributed by Joshua
• For Joshua's household is no more than for others
• For Canaanite survivors is nonexistent
• Is forfeited by adopting Canaanite ways and wives

Right of the land
• Is not entertained; the produce of the land is booty | Israel
• Had privileged rights to land as YHWH's bride
• Forfeited rights with pollution of the land

The land
• Suffers the pain of pollution and devastation
• Has a right to be purged and emptied

The elite
• In exile are promised future rights to the land
• In exile are chosen over the poor left behind |

	AGRARIAN IDEOLOGY LEVITICUS 25–27	IMMIGRANT IDEOLOGY ABRAHAM NARRATIVES
A: DOMINANT IMAGES OF THE LAND What dominant images, concepts, metaphors, and terms are used to depict the land, convey a particular orientation to the land, and thereby help to promote a given ideology?	Land as • Extended sanctuary of YHWH • Property of YHWH worked by Israelites as tenant farmers • The ʾăḥuzzah, owned property, of each tenant • Bound by sabbath principle of rest every seven years • Property to be restored in year of jubilee	Land as • Canaan, as inviting world of opportunity • As host country for immigrant groups • Terrain marked by trails and sites left by ancestors • Territory promised for future possession • Living space to be shared with host peoples • Location of sacred sites discovered by ancestors
B: LOCATION OF GOD What is the location of God in the cosmic scheme of things? What is God's position relative to the earth, the land, and the people in the land? What metaphors dominate this relationship? What is God's relative kinship with the land?	YHWH • Is local landowner, not absentee ruler in heaven • Resides in land and walks through own garden • Guarantees blessings, fertility, and harvest • Promises a double measure every sixth year	God as • El, revealed to be present at sites in the land • El, deity of the land and in the land • El Elyon, worshiped by the peoples of the land • El Shaddai, later revealed to be YHWH • El, the source of blessing and peace for the land

C: CHARTERS JUSTIFYING ENTITLEMENT TO LAND On what grounds do Israel or certain individuals or groups justify claiming entitlement to land? What stories, divine edicts, or traditions function as charters for the ideology being espoused?	The Sinai decree • Of YHWH, giving the land to Israelite tenants • Of YHWH, announcing the sabbath economy laws • Of YHWH, announcing the jubilee laws	The promise • That Abraham's seed would possess the land • Guaranteed by a treaty between God and Abraham • Symbolized by purchase of land as Sarah's burial site
D. LOCUS OF POWER IN THE LAND Where is the locus of power in the social order projected within the ideology? Whose interests are being served by the endorsement of this ideology? How is the locus of power linked to the land?	The power • Of the urban elite is removed • Of land ownership rests with peasant farmers • Over the sabbath economy resides with priests • To empty the land and give it rest lies with YHWH	The power • Of occupancy lies with the Canaanites • Is shared by sharing land • Is respected through settlements and treaties • Of blessing mediated through Abraham • As a nation promised to Abraham's seed • With Abraham as head of ancestral household or family

E. RIGHTS TO OR OF THE LAND What rights do the people, particular groups of people, or individuals have to the land? Are these rights understood in terms of justice? Are any groups excluded? Is the land itself viewed as having any rights or entitlements?	**Right to land** • Of established peasant families are pre-served • Of urban elite are negated • Of immigrants, laborers, or servants are denied • Of priests are based on law of land con-secration **Rights of the land** • Not to be exploited by continuous farming • To rest every seventh year • To be emptied and enjoy its rests	**The host peoples** • Canaanites' rights to their land are respected • Philistines' rights are respected in treaties • Hittites' rights are respected in purchase of land **Abraham** • Right to share land as immigrant, not invader • Long-term right to the land rests on land covenant • Has rights as the first head of ancestral family **The land** • Justice for the land as well as peoples

Bibliography

Ahituv, Shmuel. "Land and Justice." In *Justice and Righteousness*, edited by Henning Graf Reventlow and Yair Hoffman, 11–28. Sheffield: JSOT Press, 1992.

Amit, Yairah. "The Jubilee Law: An Attempt at Instituting Social Justice." In *Justice and Righteousness*, edited by Henning Graf Reventlow and Yair Hoffman, 47–59. Sheffield: JSOT Press, 1992.

Auld, A. G. *Joshua, Moses and the Land.* Edinburgh: Clark, 1980.

Barr, James. "Ancient Biblical Laws and Modern Human Rights." In *Justice and the Holy*, edited by D. Knight and P. Peters, 21–33. Atlanta: Scholars Press, 1989.

Benjamin, Paul. "The Theology of the Land in the Book of Joshua." Ph.D. diss., University of Chicago, 1986.

Bess, Stephen Herbert. "Systems of Land Tenure in Ancient Israel." Ph.D. diss., University of Michigan, 1963.

Brown, Arthur M. "The Concept of Inheritance in the Old Testament." Ph.D. diss., Columbia University, 1965.

Brueggemann, Walter. *The Land.* Philadelphia: Fortress, 1977.

___. "Land: Fertility and Justice." In *Theology of the Land*, edited by B. Evans and G. Cusack, 41–68. Collegeville, Minn.: Liturgical Press, 1987.

___. *Old Testament Theology: Approaches to Structure, Theme, and Text.* Minneapolis: Fortress, 1992.

Carroll, Robert. *Jeremiah: A Commentary.* Philadelphia: Westminster, 1986.

___. "The Myth of the Empty Land." *Semeia* 59 (1992): 79–93.

Catholic Commission for Justice and Peace, Uniting Church in Australia Social Responsibility and Justice Committee, and the Australian Council of Churches Commission for Church and Society. *A Just and Proper Settlement.* Blackburn: Collins Dove, 1987.

Childs, Brevard. *An Introduction to the Old Testament as Scripture.* Philadelphia: Fortress, 1979.

Clements, Ronald. "Land and Temple: A Significant Aspect of Israel's Worship." *Transactions of the Glasgow Oriental Society* 19 (1961–62): 16–28.

___. *God and Temple: The Idea of Divine Presence in Ancient Israel.* Oxford: Blackwell, 1965.

___. *Deuteronomy.* Sheffield: Academic Press, 1989.

___. *Jeremiah.* Atlanta: John Knox. 1988.

___, ed. *The World of Ancient Israel: Sociological, Anthropological and Political Perspectives.* Cambridge: Cambridge University Press, 1989.

Clifford, R. J. *The Cosmic Mountain in Canaan and the Old Testament.* Cambridge: Harvard University Press, 1972.

Coats, George. "The Ark of the Covenant in Joshua: A Probe into the History of a Tradition." *Hebrew Annual Review* 9:137–57.

Conrad, Edgar. "Re-Reading the Bible in a Multicultural World." In *Religion and Multiculturalism in Australia,* edited by Norman Habel, 324–35. Adelaide: AASR, 1992.

Coote, Robert. *Early Israel: A New Horizon.* Minneapolis: Fortress, 1990.

Cross, Frank M. *Canaanite Myth and Hebrew Epic.* Cambridge: Harvard University Press, 1973.

Davies, E. W. "Land: Its Rights and Privileges." In *The World of Ancient Israel: Sociological, Anthropological, and Political Perspectives,* edited by Ronald Clements, 349–69. Cambridge: Cambridge University Press, 1989.

Davies, W. D. *The Territorial Dimension of Judaism.* Berkeley: University of California Press, 1982.

Diepold, Peter. *Israel's Land.* Stuttgart: Kohlhammer, 1972.

Duke, R. K. "The Portion of the Levite: Another Reading of Deuteronomy 18:6-8." *JBL* 106 (1987): 193–201.

Dutcher-Walls, P. "The Social Location of the Deuteronomists." *JSOT* 52 (1991): 77–94.

Dybdahl, Jon. "Israelite Village Land Tenure: Settlement to Exile." Ph.D. diss., Fuller Theological Seminary, 1981.

Eagleton, Terry. *Criticism and Ideology: A Study in Marxist Literary Theory.* London: Verso, 1976.

Eaton, John H. *Kingship and the Psalms.* London: SCM, 1976.

Emerton, John. "The Origin of the Promises to the Patriarchs in the Older Sources of the Book of Genesis." *VT* 32 (1982): 14–32.

Eslinger, Lyle. *Into the Hands of the Living God.* Sheffield: Almond, 1989.

Fager, Jeffrey. "Land Tenure and the Biblical Jubilee: A Moral World View." Ph.D. diss., Vanderbilt University, 1987.

___. *Land Tenure and the Biblical Jubilee: Uncovering Hebrew Ethics through the Sociology of Knowledge.* Sheffield: JSOT Press, 1993.

Fishbane, Michael. "Jeremiah 4:23-26 and Job 3:3-13: A Recovered Use of the Creation Pattern." *VT* 21 (1971): 151–67.

Fontaine, Carole. "The Bearing of Wisdom on the Shape of 2 Samuel 11–12 and 1 Kings 3." *JSOT* 34 (1986): 61–77.

Forshey, R. O. "The Hebrew Root *NHL* and Its Semitic Cognates." Ph.D. diss., Harvard University, 1972.

Garbini, Giovanni. *History and Ideology in Ancient Israel.* New York: Crossroad, 1988.

Geertz, Clifford. "Ideology as a Cultural System." In *Ideology and Discontent,* edited by David E. Apter, 47–76. New York: Free Press, 1964.

Gerleman, Gillis. "Nutzrecht und Wohnrecht: zur Bedeutung von 'Achuzah und Nachalah.'" *ZAW* 89 (1977): 313–25.

Gnuse, Robert. "Jubilee Legislation in Leviticus: Israel's Vision of Social Reform." *Biblical Theology Bulletin* 15 (1985): 43–48.

Görg, Manfred. *Gott-König-Reden in Israel und Ägypten.* Stuttgart: Kohlhammer, 1975.

Gottwald, Norman. *The Tribes of Yahweh: A Sociology of the Religion of Liberated Israel, 1250–1050 B.C.* Maryknoll, N.Y.: Orbis, 1979.

___. "Social Class and Ideology in Isaiah 40–55: An Eagletonian Reading." *Semeia* 59 (1992): 43–57.

Gray, John. *I & II Kings: A Commentary.* Philadelphia: Westminster, 1964.

Gunn, David M. "Joshua and Judges." In *The Literary Guide to the Bible,* edited by Robert Alter and Frank Kermode, 102–21. Cambridge: Harvard University, Belknap Press, 1987.

Haag, E. "Die Abrahamtradition in Gen. 15." In *Die Vaeter Israels,* edited by A. R. Mueller and M. Görg, 83–106. Stuttgart: Katholisches Bibelwerk, 1989.

Habel, Norman. *Yahweh Versus Baal.* New York: Bookman Associates, 1964.

___. "Conquest and Dispossession: Justice, Joshua and Land Rights." *Pacifica* 4 (1991): 76–92.

___. "Peoples at Peace: The Land Ideology of the Abraham Narratives." In *Religion and Multiculturalism in Australia,* edited by Norman Habel, 336–49. Adelaide: AASR, 1992.

___. "The Suffering Land: Ideology in Jeremiah," *Lutheran Theological Journal* 26 (1992): 14–26.

Halpern, Baruch. "The Centralisation Formula in Deuteronomy." *VT* 31 (1981): 20–38.

Hamlin, E. John. "The Joshua Tradition Reinterpreted." *South East Asian Journal of Theology* 23 (1982) :103–8.

Hawk, L. Daniel. *Every Promise Fulfilled: Contesting Plots in Joshua.* Louisville: Westminster/John Knox, 1991.

Herrmann, Siegfried. "Die Königsnovelle in Agypten und Israel." *Wissenschaftliche Zeitschrift der Karl Marx Universität Leipzig* 3 (1953): 51–62.

Hill, Andrew. "The Ebal Ceremony as Hebrew Land Grant?" *JETS* 31 (1988): 399–406.

Hobbs, T. R. "Reflections on 'the Poor' and the Old Testament." *The Expository Times* 100 (1989): 291–94.

Hopkins, David. *The Highlands of Canaan: Agricultural Life in the Early Iron Age.* Sheffield: Almond, 1985.

Hoppe, L. *Being Poor: A Biblical Study.* New York: Glazier, 1987.

Horst, Friedrich. "Zwei Begriffe für Eigentum (Besitz): *nahala* und *ʾaḥuzza.*" In *Verbannung und Heimkehr,* edited by A. Fuschke, 135–56. Tübingen: J. C. B. Mohr, 1966.

"Ideological Criticism of Biblical Texts," *Semeia* 59 (1992).

Jeyaraj, Jesudason. "Land Ownership in the Pentateuch." Ph.D. diss., University of Sheffield, 1989.

___. "Siding with the Landless." In *The Gospel in the Modern World: A Tribute to John Stott,* edited by Martyn Eden and David Wells. Downers Grove, Ill.: Intervarsity Press, 1991.

___. "Ownership, Tenancy and Care of Land in Leviticus 25–27." Typescript.

Jobling, David. "Forced Labor: Solomon's Golden Age and the Question of Literary Representation." *Semeia* 54 (1991): 57–76.

___. "Deconstruction and the Political Analysis of Biblical Texts: A Jamesonian Reading of Psalm 72." *Semeia* 59 (1992): 95–127.

Johnstone, W. "Old Testament Technical Expressions in Property Holding: Contributions from Ugarit." *Ugaritica* 6 (1969).

Koopmans, William. *Joshua 24 as Poetic Narrative.* Sheffield: JSOT Press, 1992.

Kraus, Hans Joachim. *The Theology of the Psalms.* Minneapolis: Augsburg, 1986.

Lang, Bernhard. "The Social Organisation of Peasant Poverty in Biblical Israel." *JSOT* 24 (1983): 47–63.

Lemche, Niels Peter. *Early Israel: Anthropological and Historical Studies on Israelite Society before the Monarchy.* Leiden: Brill, 1985.

___. *The Canaanites and Their Land: The Tradition of the Canaanites.* Sheffield: JSOT Press, 1991.

Lilburne, Geoffrey. *A Sense of Place: A Christian Theology of Land.* Nashville: Abingdon, 1989.

Mannheim, Karl. *Ideology and Utopia.* New York: Harcourt Brace Jovanovich, 1985.

Mayes, A. D. H. "On Describing the Purpose of Deuteronomy." *JSOT* 59 (1993): 13–33.

McBride, S. Dean. "Polity of the Covenant People." *Interpretation* 41 (1987): 229–44.

McCarthy, Dennis. "The Theology of Leadership in Joshua 1–9." *Biblica* 52 (1971): 165–75.

___. *Treaty and Covenant.* Rome: Biblical Institute Press, 1978.

McConville, John G. *Law and Theology in Deuteronomy.* Sheffield: JSOT Press, 1984.

___. "1 Chronicles 28:9: Yahweh 'Seeks Out' Solomon." *JTS* 37 (1986): 105–8.

McKnight, Edgar V. *Post-Modern Use of the Bible: The Emergence of Reader-Oriented Criticism.* Nashville: Abingdon, 1988.

___. "Reader Perspectives on the New Testament." *Semeia* 48 (1989): 1–206.

Mendenhall, George. "The Nature and Purpose of the Abraham Narratives." In *Ancient Israelite Religion,* edited by Patrick Miller et al., 337–56. Philadelphia: Fortress, 1987.

Mettinger, Tryggve. *Solomonic State Officials: A Study of the Civil Government Officials of the Israelite Monarchy.* Lund: Gleerup, 1971.

___. *King and Messiah: The Civil and Sacral Legitimation of the Israelite Kings.* Lund: Gleerup, 1976.

Meyers, Carol. "The Israelite Empire: In Defense of King Solomon." In *The Bible and Its Traditions,* edited by M. P. O'Connor and D. N. Freedman, 421–28. Michigan University Press, 1983.

___. "'To Her Mother's House': Considering a Counterpart to the Israelite *bet ʾab.*" In *The Bible and the Politics of Exegesis,* edited by David Jobling et al., 39–51. Cleveland: Pilgrim, 1992.

Miller, Patrick D. "The Gift of God: The Deuteronomic Theology of the Land." *Interpretation* 23 (1969): 451–65.

Miscall, P. *The Workings of Old Testament Narrative.* Chico, Calif.: Scholars Press, 1983.

Naday, Na'aman. "The District System of Israel in the Time of the United Monarchy" (in Hebrew). *Zion* 48 (1983): 1–20.

Nelson, R. "Josiah in the Book of Joshua." *JBL* 100 (1981): 531–40.

Niehaus, Jeffrey. "Joshua and Ancient Near Eastern Warfare." *JETS* 31 (1988): 37–50.

North, Robert. *Sociology of the Biblical Jubilee.* Rome: Pontifical Biblical Institute, 1954.

Noth, Martin. *Exodus.* Philadelphia: Westminster, 1962.

O'Brien, Mark. "The 'Deuteronomistic History' as a Story of Israel's Leaders." *Australian Biblical Review* 37 (1989): 14–34.

___. "Authority in Israel: The Deuteronomic Contribution in Deut. 16:18—18:22." Paper presented at International SBL Conference.

Orlinsky, Harry M. "The Biblical Concept of the Land of Israel:

Cornerstone of the Covenant between God and Israel." In *The Land of Israel: Jewish Perspectives,* edited by L. A. Hoffman, 27–64. Notre Dame, Ind.: University of Notre Dame Press, 1986.

Ottosson, Magnus. *Josuaboken: en Programskrift for Davidsk Restauration.* Stockholm: Almqvist & Wiksell, 1991.

Parker, Kim. "Wisdom and Law in the Reign of Solomon." Ph.D. diss., McMaster University, 1989.

Perlitt, Lothar. "Motive und Schichten der Landtheologie im Deuteronomium." In *Das Land Israels in biblischer Zeit,* edited by G. Strecker, 46–58. Göttingen: Vandenhoeck & Ruprecht, 1983.

Phillips, Anthony. *Ancient Israel's Criminal Law: A New Approach to the Decalogue.* Oxford: Blackwell, 1970.

Polley, Max. *Amos and the Davidic Empire: A Socio-Historical Approach.* Oxford: Oxford University Press, 1989.

Polzin, Robert. *Moses and the Deuteronomist.* New York: Seabury, 1980.

Premnath, D. N. "Latifundialization and Isaiah 5:8-10." *JSOT* 40 (1988): 49–60.

Preris, Aloysius. *An Asian Theology of Liberation.* Maryknoll, N.Y.: Orbis, 1988.

Ricoeur, Paul. *Lectures on Ideology and Utopia.* New York: Columbia University Press, 1986.

Ringe, Sharon. *Jesus, Liberation and the Biblical Jubilee: Images for Ethics and Christology.* Philadelphia: Fortress, 1985.

Rodgers, Margaret. "Luke 4:16-30: A Call for a Jubilee Year?" *Reformed Theological Review* 40 (1981): 72–82.

Rofe, Alexander. "The Vineyard of Naboth: The Origin and Message of the Story." *VT* 38 (1988): 89–104.

Rubinger, N. J. "Jeremiah's Epistle to the Exiles and the Field in Anathoth." *Judaism* 26 (1977): 84–91.

Scharbert, J. "Die Landverheissung an die Väter als einfache Zusage, als Eid and als 'Bund.'" In *Konsequente Traditionsgeschichte.* Göttingen: Vandenhoeck & Ruprecht, 1993.

Shils, E. "Ideology: The Concept and Function of Ideology." In *International Encyclopedia of Social Sciences,* edited by David Sills. Vol. 7, 66–75. New York: Macmillan Co., 1968.

Soggin, J. Alberto. "Compulsory Labor under David and Solomon." In

Studies in the Period of David and Solomon, edited by Tomoo Ishida, 259–67. Winona Lake, Ind.: Eisenbrauns, 1982.

Spina, Frank. "Israelites as *gerim,* 'Sojourners,' in Social and Historical Context." In *The Word of the Lord Shall Go Forth,* edited by Carol Meyers and M. O'Connor, 321–35. Winona Lake, Ind.: Eisenbrauns, 1983.

Stager, L. E. "The Archaeology of the Family in Ancient Israel." *BASOR* 260 (1985): 1–35.

Sternberg, M. *The Poetics of Biblical Narrative: Ideological Literature and the Drama of Reading.* Bloomington: Indiana University Press, 1985.

Stone, Lawson. "Ethical and Apologetic Tendencies in the Redaction of the Book of Joshua." *Catholic Biblical Quarterly* 53 (1991): 25–35.

Strehlow, T. G. H. *Aranda Traditions.* Melbourne: Melbourne University Press, 1947.

Sutherland, Ray. "Israelite Political Theory in Joshua 9." *JSOT* 53 (1992): 65–74.

Thiel, W. *Die deuteronomische Redaktion von Jeremia 1–25.* Neukirchen-Vluyn: Neukirchener Verlag, 1981.

Thompson, John B. *Studies in the Theory of Ideology.* Cambridge: Polity Press, 1984.

Thompson, Kenneth. *Beliefs and Ideologies.* London: Tavistock, 1986.

Thompson, Thomas. *Early History of the Israelite People: From the Written and Archaeological Sources.* Leiden: E. J. Brill, 1992.

Van Houten, Christiana. *The Alien in Israelite Law.* Sheffield: Sheffield Academic Press, 1991.

Van Seters, John. *Abraham in History and Tradition.* New Haven: Yale University Press, 1975.

___. "Joshua 24 and the Problem of Tradition in the Old Testament." In *In the Shelter of Elyon: Essays on Ancient Palestinian Life and Literature,* edited by W. Barrick and J. Spencer, 139–58. Sheffield: JSOT Press, 1984.

___. *Prologue to History: The Yahwist as Historian in Genesis.* Louisville: Westminster/John Knox, 1992.

Von Rad, Gerhard. *Old Testament Theology.* Vol. 1. Edinburgh: Oliver & Boyd, 1962.

___. "The Promised Land and Yahweh's Land in the Hexateuch." In

The Problem of the Hexateuch and Other Essays, edited by Gerhard von Rad, 79–93. New York: McGraw-Hill, 1966.

Von Weimar, Peter. "Gen. 17 und die priesterschriftliche Abrahamgeschichte." *ZAW* 100 (1988): 22–60.

Wang, M. Chen-Chang. "Jeremiah's Message of Hope in Prophetic Symbolic Action." *South-East Asia Journal of Theology* 14 (1972).

Weinberg, Joel P. "Die Agrärverhältnisse in der Burger-Temple-Gemeinde der Achamenidenzeit." *Acta Antiqua* 22 (1974): 473–86.

Weinfeld, Moshe. "Divine Intervention in War in Ancient Israel and in the Ancient Near East." In *History, Historiography and Interpretation,* edited by Hayim Tadmore and Moshe Weinfeld, 121–47. Jerusalem: Magnes Press, 1983.

____. "Sabbatical Year and Jubilee in the Pentateuchal Laws and Their Ancient Near Eastern Background." In *The Law in the Bible and Its Environment,* edited by Timo Veijola, 39–62. Göttingen: Vandenhoeck & Ruprecht, 1990.

Wenham, Gordon. "The Deuteronomic Theology of the Book of Joshua." *JBL* 90 (1971): 140–48.

Westbrook, Raymond. "Redemption of Land." *Israel Land Review* 6 (1971): 368–69.

____. *Property and Family in Biblical Law.* Sheffield: JSOT Press, 1991.

Westermann, Claus. *The Promise to the Fathers: Studies on the Patriarchal Narratives.* Philadelphia: Fortress, 1980.

____. *Genesis 12–36.* London: SPCK, 1985.

Whitelam, Keith. *The Just King: Monarchical Judicial Authority in Ancient Israel.* Sheffield: JSOT Press, 1980.

____. "The Symbols of Power: Aspects of Royal Propaganda in the United Monarchy." *Biblical Archaeologist* 49 (1986): 166–73.

____. "Israelite Kingship: The Royal Ideology and Its Opponents." In *The World of Ancient Israel,* edited by Ronald Clements, 119–39. Cambridge: Cambridge University Press, 1989.

____. "Israel's Traditions of Origin: Reclaiming the Land." *JSOT* 44 (1989): 19–42.

Wielenga, Bastiaan. *It's a Long Road to Freedom: Perspectives on Biblical Theology.* Madurai: Tamil Nadu Theological Seminary, 1981.

Wittenberg, Gunther. "The Significance of Land in the Old Testament." *Journal for Theology in South Africa* 77 (1991): 58–60.

Wolff, Hans Walther. "The Kerygma of the Yahwist." In *The Vitality of the Old Testament Traditions,* edited by Walter Brueggemann and Hans Walther Wolff, 41–66. Atlanta: John Knox, 1975.

Wright, Christopher J. H. *God's People in God's Land: Family, Land and Property in the Old Testament.* Grand Rapids: Wm. B. Eerdmans Publishing Co., 1990.

Younger, K. Lawson. *Ancient Conquest Accounts: A Study of Ancient Near Eastern and Biblical History Writing.* Sheffield: JSOT Press, 1990.

___. "The Figurative Aspect and the Contextual Method in the Evaluation of the Solomonic Empire (1 Kings 1–11)." In *The Bible in Three Dimensions,* edited by David Clines et al., 157–75. Sheffield: JSOT Press, 1990.

Zimmerli, Walther. "The 'Land' in the Pre-Exilic and Early Post-Exilic Prophets." In *Understanding the Word,* edited by James Butler et al. Sheffield: JSOT Press, 1985.

Index of

Scripture References

Index of
Hebrew Terms

Index of Authors

176

Index of Subjects

Aaron, 48, 59
Abimelech, 119, 128, 130
  as land-giver, 128
Aboriginal Australians, xiii, 2, 4, 7
  Aranda, 1
Abraham, 9, 11, 59, 88, 132
  ancestral hero, 118, 129, 130
  and covenant entitlement, 125, 133
  and exodus, 124
  and god of land, 130, 131-32, 146
  and Jeremiah, 88, 91
  and justice, 128, 129, 133
  and land, 120, 122, 124, 125, 146, 148
  and Lot, 118, 126, 129
  and Melchizedek, 126, 146
  and relationship with land, 148
  and sacred sites, 119
  and sharing the land, 125, 126, 130, 146
  and subsequent land claims, 124, 139
  and YHWH, 117, 121, 123, 126, 131-32, 139
  as alien, 129
  as ancestral leader, 127, 130, 132, 133, 146
  as dealing justly with land, 133
  as first to take possession of land, 124
  as herder, 138
  as immigrant, 116, 118, 119, 124, 125, 126, 129, 131, 133, 136, 146, 148
    See also Ger
  as interceder, 127
  as land surveyor, 119, 126
  as led by God, 118
  as mediator of blessing, 120, 121, 122, 125, 126, 127, 128, 129, 133, 146
  as member of divine council, 132
  as model of righteousness, 128

  as model peacemaker, 125, 127, 128, 129, 130, 133, 136, 146
  as paradigm of a leader, 121
  as priest, 132
  as progenitor of great nation, 120, 121
  as prophet, 128
  as rescuer, 126
  attitude to Canaanites, 125, 126, 127, 129, 130, 132, 133, 146
  attitude to Hittites, 129
  blessing of, 126, 132, 139, 146
  burial plot as symbol, 129, 133, 142
  charter promise of, 124, 142
  entitlement to land, 123, 124, 133, 142, 146
  faith of, 123
  great name of, 120
  intimate god of, 132
  land plot as down payment, 123
  narratives of, 8, 9, 16, 91, 115-19, 135, 136, 138, 148
  relations with people of the land, 129, 130, 132, 133, 146
  seed of, 119, 142
    Beer-sheba and, 128
Adultery metaphor, 81
Agrarian land ideology
  See Land ideology, agrarian
Ahab, 30-31
Aliens, resident
  See Immigrants
Allotment
  See Land, as allotment
Amnesty, economic
Amos, 83
  Book of, 11
Ancestors, 70-71, 73, 115

Day of Atonement
  See Atonement, day of
De-creation, 87
Defilement
  See Land, pollution of
Deuteronomic
  editor, 62
  framework, 143
  history, 54
  monarch, 67
  reform, 48
Deuteronomy
  Book of, 5, 36, 127, 134, 137, 139, 140,
    141
  land ideology of, 36-53
  militant ideology of, 127
  polity of, 37-39, 47
Dialogical approach to text, 7

Earth, as cosmic empire, 27
Ecojustice, 7
El, 130, 131, 136, 139, 146
El Elyon, 77, 126, 131, 139, 146
El Olam, 129, 131, 139
El Shaddai, 131, 139
Elijah, 31
Empty land
  See Land, as empty
Enemy from the North, 86
Exile, from land, 9, 52, 75, 89, 95, 96,
    113, 116, 117, 130, 136, 139, 140,
    145
  and land rights, 144
  and sabbath, 113
  conditions for return from, 50, 95
  conditions leading to, 52, 61, 80, 83,
    113, 139, 140, 147
  elite and, 93, 94, 96, 144, 145
  fig imagery, 89
  return from, 55, 75, 89, 91, 92, 94, 123
  strategy for survival in, 89, 92
Exodus, the, 38, 69, 82, 109, 123, 131
Ezekiel, 31

Family, line of, 69
  See also Ancestral household
Fertility
  and blessing, 122
  cults, 81
  deities of, 45, 86
  of land, 46, 78, 122
  rites of, 77, 80, 82
  source of
    See YHWH, as source of fertility

Forced laborers
  See Corvée labor; Slaves
Foreign gods
  See Gods of Canaan

Gibeonites, 60, 61, 71
Give (*ntn*), as legal term, 39-40, 52
God
  abode as vineyard, 79
  and imagery, 137
  and land, 138
  and other gods, 45, 61
  as creator, 87
  as creator of cosmos, 137
  as El, El Olam, El Elyon, El Shaddai,
    131
  as god of the land, Canaan, 116, 119,
    130-32
  as god of the promise, 123
  as host deity, 124
  as landgiver, 25
  as monarch, 27
  as owner of the land, 130
  as powerful being, 137
  as redeemer, 89
  as sovereign in heaven, 25
  as sufferer, 87
  as warrior, 71
  as welcoming host, 119
  as YHWH, 123
  comparison with monarchs, 138
  creates and rules by decree, 138
  fear of, 128, 131
  function of, 137-39
  habitation in heaven, 26, 137
  hierarchical relationship to land, 138
  image of, given to Abraham, 116
  location of, 14, 25, 26, 27, 137-39, 147
  nahalah as garden/vineyard, 79
  relationship with land, 14, 137
    See also Land, God, people
  rules through monarch, 137
    See also Monarch
    See also YHWH
Gods of Canaan, 45, 61, 73, 123
Golden age, 22
  of Solomon
    See Solomon, golden age of
Grace of YHWH
  See YHWH

Hagar, 130
Heads
  See Leaders

Lightning Source UK Ltd.
Milton Keynes UK
UKHW021705130720
366460UK00006B/1036